WORD
BIBLICAL
THEMES

———General Editor———
David A. Hubbard

———Old Testament Editor———
John D. W. Watts

———New Testament Editor———
Ralph P. Martin

WORD
BIBLICAL
THEMES

John

GEORGE R. BEASLEY-MURRAY

WORD PUBLISHING
Dallas · London · Sydney · Singapore

JOHN
Word Biblical Themes

Scripture quotations in this volume from the book of John, unless otherwise indicated, are from the author's translation in *John*, Volume 36, of the Word Biblical Commentary, copyrighted 1987 by Word, Incorporated. See the Index for abbreviations for other versions used in this volume.

Library of Congress Cataloging-in-Publication Data

Beasley-Murray, George Raymond, 1916–
    John / George R. Beasley-Murray.
       p.   cm. — (Word Biblical themes)
    Includes index.
    ISBN 0-8499-0624-5
    1. Bible. N.T. John—Criticism, interpretation, etc. I. Title.
II. Series.
BS2615.2.B385   1989
226'.507—dc19
                                         89-5299
                                        CIP

Printed in the United States of America
9 8 0 1 2 3 9 RRD 9 8 7 6 5 4 3 2 1

To P. H. Warwick Bailey
my first pastor,
through whom I learned of Christ

CONTENTS

FOREWORD

Already George Beasley-Murray's *John* in the *Word Biblical Commentary* series has been hailed as a monumental study of the "spiritual Gospel." Scholars and students are discovering fresh insights and penetrating observations on this central New Testament book. Not all readers today, however, are interested in the minutiae of the academic debate on the fourth Gospel. Rather, they are looking for guidance on the leading themes of John as material for pulpit messages, Bible-class themes, and practical daily living.

This book in the continuing series of *Word Biblical Themes* is designed expressly for a general audience, especially busy pastors and preachers and layfolk who want to be informed by the most reliable teachers of the church.

Dr. Beasley-Murray brings to his assignment a wealth of past experience—as minister of a local congregation for many years, then seminary principal in charge of the famed Spurgeon's College in London, and later professor at Southern Baptist Theological Seminary in Louisville, Kentucky.

Now retired from these key posts, he still is active in

preaching and teaching. He is eminently qualified to offer this study on John which distills and puts into succinct form the massive research of his larger commentary. Dr. Beasley-Murray works with an eye always on his audience which will appreciate his easy style and helpful approach to this Gospel.

No one can fail to profit from his latest work.

Department of Biblical Studies   Ralph P. Martin
The University of Sheffield   New Testament Editor
                                       Word Biblical Themes,
                                       Word Biblical Commentary

PREFACE

Anyone who is concerned to gain an understanding of the Christian faith will pay special attention to the four Gospels, in the endeavor to learn something sure about Jesus. This has been true of the present writer. On reflection, however, he realizes that the Gospel of John has occupied a unique place in his thinking, his life, his preaching, and his teaching. In his experience theological students find this book to be of unparalleled interest, including even its complex background, which throws a flood of light on the story it records. People in the churches are similarly fascinated when the unsuspected depths of the Gospel are uncovered and explained to them. John's Gospel is the preacher's Gospel *par excellence*. It is therefore the more regrettable that preaching and teaching about this Gospel often remains on a superficial level and ignores much that lies waiting to be discovered and proclaimed.

This little book is intended to be a kind of mini-handbook to the profoundest book of the Bible, to help preachers and teachers to grasp its message and worthily to make it known. Hopefully it may stimulate some to resort to the great commentaries that have been written on the Gospel, and so lead to the satisfaction of attaining a fuller understanding of the so-called "spiritual Gospel."

Chapter 5, on the Upper Room Discourses of Jesus, reproduces the substance of an article which appeared in the *Review and Expositor*, volume 85, 1968, pp. 473–83; the writer expresses his gratitude to the editor for permission to utilize it.

George R. Beasley-Murray

1 INTERPRETING THE GOSPEL OF JOHN

Ever since the church realized that it possesses not one Gospel but four it has come to see that the Gospel of John is "different." Something about its presentation of Jesus marks it off from the others, and makes it unique. A great deal of discussion about this difference has taken place in modern times. It used to be said that whereas Matthew, Mark, and Luke gave the bare facts of the story of Jesus, John gave us the facts plus interpretation. We now know that that is an overstatement. Each of the first three evangelists had his own understanding of Jesus, and each wrote up his account in order that the light of Christ might shed its maximum illumination upon the circumstances of the churches he knew. Those men had profound insight into the life and teaching of Jesus and the revelation of God that he brought.

Yet everyone who has considered the matter agrees that these observations apply to the fourth evangelist and his Gospel in a very special way. One has only to pick up the book and read its opening sentences to realize what a unique slant the evangelist gives to the familiar story of Jesus. There is something paradoxical about the introduction to this Gospel (1:1-18). It is written in the simplest language possible. Indeed, the first five verses are not only in "basic Greek," to coin an expression in imitation of "basic English"; a beginner who has taken only his first steps in learning the language can make out those sentences. And yet the significance of its utterances about Jesus is nothing less than breathtaking. The Prologue plumbs the depths and scales the heights of the doctrine of Christ beyond anything written in the Bible. It unveils the central place of the Son of God in revelation, in creation, and in redemption; and it relates all this not only to the record of God's revelation in the Old Testament but also to the religions and philosophies of the ancient world from primeval times to the fashionable thought of the evangelist's day.

One of the greatest teachers of the early church, Clement of Alexandria, who was acquainted with the thought of the world of the second century of our era, wrote about this book: "John, perceiving that the bodily facts had been made plain in the gospel, being urged by his friends and inspired by the Spirit, composed a spiritual gospel."[1]

It will be observed that in that statement there is no consciousness of opposition between the "spiritual Gospel" and the earlier Gospels. The so-called Muratorian Canon, a report on the books of the New Testament composed in the period of Clement's ministry, elaborates what Clement said of the fourth Gospel, and then adds:

> Although various points are taught in the several books of the gospels, yet it makes no difference to the faith of believers, since all things in all of them are declared by one supreme Spirit.

That is a perceptive statement. The differences between the accounts of Jesus in the synoptic Gospels and that in John are

acknowledged, but the four accounts are seen to be complementary, and the varied interpretations are ascribed to the
operation of the "one supreme Spirit."

Once more, this aspect of the composition of the Gospels is
especially apparent in John, which has more to say about the
work of the Holy Spirit in the church than any of the other
Gospels; and this Gospel specifically relates that work of the
Spirit to the understanding of the words and deeds of Jesus.

We think, for example, of the statement of Jesus to the
disciples in the Upper Room: "I have spoken these things
while remaining with you; but the Counselor, the Holy
Spirit, whom the Father will send in my name, will teach you
everything, and will remind you of everything that I have said
to you" (John 14:25, 26). The Spirit, then, has the dual task of
bringing to remembrance what Jesus has said and of instructing the disciples as to its meaning. That is precisely what we
have in this "spiritual Gospel"—*reminiscence* of the works
and words of Jesus as *interpreted by the Spirit*.

Our major task, accordingly, is to seek to interpret by the
Spirit this interpretation of Jesus from the Spirit. All other
issues in the investigation of the Gospel are subordinate to
this supreme concern. It is well to recognize this at the outset,
for in any case there is a great deal of uncertainty about many
matters which people like to know about a book, for example, who wrote it, when it was written, where and for whom it
was written, and the like. In particular, endless argument has
taken place over the identity of the author of John. Books
and articles have been devoted to it, sometimes with a ve-
hemence suggesting that the validity and authority of the
message of the book stand or fall with its traditional ascription of authorship to the apostle John.

In reality, this Gospel, like the others, is anonymous; it
would be preposterous to commit ourselves to the view that
the authority of our four Gospels depends on the accuracy
of the ascription of their authorship by churches in the

second century. The truth of their message depends on their connection with Jesus and the guidance of the Holy Spirit given both to those who handed on the facts and their meaning and the evangelists themselves. In the case of our Gospel there is clear indication of the activity of the Spirit alike in maintaining, understanding, and declaring the story of Jesus, and this the church has thankfully recognized through the ages.

Authorship

We have said that the fourth Gospel is anonymous. There is no mention of the author's *name*, in contrast to Paul's writings or the book of Revelation (Rev 1:1, 4, 9). There is, however, an additional chapter, written after the Gospel had been brought to its completion (at 20:30, 31), in which a statement as to the source of the Gospel is made. After recounting the Easter conversation of Jesus with Peter a reference is made to "the disciple whom Jesus loved," and then it is affirmed: "This is the disciple who bears witness about these things and who wrote these things, and we know that his witness is true" (21:24).

The statement calls forth two observations. First, the disciple's *name* is not stated, nor is it given anywhere else in the Gospel: we shall return to this issue shortly. Secondly, the natural inference from the assertion is that the writer is speaking of "the disciple whom Jesus loved" as someone *other than himself*, exactly as in 19:35: "The man who saw this has borne witness to it—and his witness is authentic, and he knows that he tells the truth—that you, too, may believe." In both passages the disciple is cited as an independent witness whose testimony is authentic; but in this passage the distinction between writer and disciple is emphasized: "We who know the man know that he is a reliable witness." When, therefore, it is stated that the beloved disciple "wrote" these things, it must mean that he wrote down *his witness*. That is the point of emphasis in the sentence. And although the writer does not explicitly say so, he certainly implies that the written testimony of the beloved disciple is the source and the authority of what is written in this Gospel.

This is confirmed by the way the author speaks about the man who stands behind this Gospel. He calls him "the disciple whom Jesus loved." Since it is made clear that Jesus loved all his disciples (cf. 13:1, 2; 15:12-15) the expression must mean "the disciple whom Jesus *especially* loved." There was an affinity between Jesus and this man beyond that between Jesus and the rest of the disciples. The first occasion when the expression is used is peculiarly instructive. Jesus had declared that one of the disciples was to betray him; Peter therefore made signs to "the disciple whom Jesus loved" to ask who it was, for the Beloved Disciple was "close to the breast of Jesus" (13:23). The expression is literally "in the bosom of Jesus." This physical position was possible because Jesus and the disciple group were reclining round the low table, with elbows on cushions, according to the custom of celebrating the Passover. The Beloved Disciple was reclining next to Jesus, and as host, Jesus was slightly forward. The disciple had but to turn toward Jesus and his head would then have been on his chest, and a whispered conversation could take place.

But the expression "in the bosom of" has a counterpart in the Prologue. It is written, "God no one has ever seen. The only Son, by nature God, *who is ever close to the Father's heart*, has brought knowledge of him" (1:18). The expression "close to the heart of . . ." is the same as in 13:24, "in the bosom of . . . ," i.e., in closest intimacy with the Father. The evangelist evidently wished to convey the thought that just as Jesus was and is in closest fellowship with the Father, and therefore has been able to reveal God as none other before or since him, so the disciple whom Jesus loved was in closest intimacy with Jesus and has been able to reveal the truth he brought as no

Interpreting the Gospel of John

other person could. Whereas it is perfectly understandable that one who knew that disciple well should so speak about him, it would be incomprehensible for the disciple himself to describe himself in this way and imply such a comparison with the rest of the disciples.

Who then was the favored disciple? Irenaeus, bishop of Lyons in the last quarter of the second century, named him as the apostle John ("John, the disciple of the Lord, who leaned on his breast, also published the gospel while living in Ephesus in Asia").[2] It is perfectly possible that the identification is correct. That would mean that the apostle John was the authority behind the Gospel that has so long borne his name.

But there are difficulties about this. Various things said about the apostle John in the early tradition are unlikely to be true, as, for example, when he is said to have written the Gospel after the death of the emperor Domitian (i.e., after the year A.D. 98 and after his release from Patmos, when he pursued an active ministry in the churches of Asia Minor). The apostle in the years A.D. 100 and later would have been about a hundred years old! The beloved disciple was certainly a *friend of Peter*. If, as is likely, he was "the other disciple" with Peter, mentioned in 18:15, 16 (cf. the use of that expression in 20:2, 3, 5, 8), then he was also a *friend of Caiaphas*, the high priest. That is explicitly stated in verses 18:15, 16. And that was how he was known to the woman who kept the gate of the high priest's courtyard (18:15f). He will then have been a member of the high-priestly circle of Jerusalem. That explains how it is that this Gospel gives so much information about the ministry of Jesus in Jerusalem and Judea, of which the other Gospels know nothing, and in particular how he knew so much about the trial of Jesus before Pilate. The Gospel is written from the viewpoint of a resident of Judea (probably of Jerusalem) in contrast with the synoptic Gospels, which convey the witness of followers of Jesus in Galilee.

We cannot pretend to be able to solve this issue. The Christians for whom the Gospel was written would have known the beloved disciple so well, they did not need telling who he was. We must be satisfied to know that he was privileged to be exceptionally close to Jesus, and therefore exceptionally well acquainted with the thought of Jesus. He was enabled by the Spirit not only to grasp what he heard and saw but to pass on to the churches that understanding of Jesus; and the Lord gave him a disciple of like mind, similarly illuminated by the Spirit, who was led to set down in writing for all subsequent generations the knowledge of him which is life eternal (17:3).

Purpose

This leads on to the *purpose* of the fourth Gospel. The evangelist himself has stated it in the intended conclusion, namely 20:30, 31: "Now there were many other signs that Jesus did in the presence of his disciples that are not recorded in this book; but these have been written so that you may believe that Jesus is the Christ, the Son of God, and that through believing you may have life in his name." It is possible to interpret these words in two ways: the Gospel was written that people who have not come to faith in Jesus as the Christ and Son of God may do so, and thereby gain the life of the kingdom of God; or, the Gospel was written that those who believe in Jesus may have their faith deepened, and grasp more fully its truth and its implications. Thereby they should experience in fuller measure the life of the kingdom now and be assured of possessing its fullness in the coming age.

The curious thing is that there is a difference of spelling of the verb "believe" in our earliest manuscripts, one form favoring the former interpretation and the other the latter. We cannot be certain which reading is right, but in any case

Interpreting the Gospel of John

either reading can be understood in either way! Irrespective of that conundrum, the nature of the Gospel itself suggests that there is no need to settle for an either/or here. The Gospel has both an evangelistic thrust and a deeply instructive quality. It has power to awaken faith and to confirm faith, and was surely intended for use in mission to those outside the churches and for building up those inside them.

With regard to the latter purpose, the churches for which the evangelist wrote needed guidance in dealing with various groups of religious people with whom they rubbed shoulders. Some of these were in sympathy with the gospel, and some far from it. There are some ambiguous references to John the Baptist in the Gospel, which speak appreciatively of John's unique role as witness to Jesus and at the same time emphasize his secondary place to Jesus regarding the revelation and salvation of God. This is seen with special clarity in John 1:6-9 and in 3:25-30. These passages may well have in view the contemporary followers of John the Baptist, who claimed that John was the Light of men and the Redeemer from God (these claims were actually made in later years by the Mandaeans, some of whom exist to this day). The evangelist deals gently and tactfully with this issue, in view of the honor in which John was held by Jesus and by the church after him.

It is likely that John also had his eyes on the "Gnostics," whose name means "the people who know." Their views swept the nearer Orient in the second century, but it is evident that they were spreading in the first century also. The system was syncretistic, a mishmash of religion and philosophy, at the root of which was a dualistic view of reality. They believed that all that is material is evil and that only what is spirit is good, a view congenial to the Eastern mind, and which has sometimes infected Christianity. Carried to its extreme this doctrine effectively divides God from the world, which in any case he could not have created, since (on this view) it is evil. It similarly makes the Incarnation of the Son of God impossible, for he could not have adopted a material body; and it further changed redemption to deliverance from the material world rather than from sin.

But there were different degrees of approximation to this kind of teaching. The paradoxical thing is that many Gnostics were drawn to the Gospel of John. The first commentary on the Gospel known to us was written by Basilides, a Gnostic!—and it became the instrument in the hands of the church to oppose Gnosticism in the second century. The truth is that many of the Gnostics were not far from the kingdom of God, to use an expression of Jesus (Mark 12:34), as we now know from the Nag Hammadi collection of Gnostic works recently discovered in Egypt.

It is likely that the evangelist was acquainted with more than one sort of Gnostic, and that he wrote with a view to helping those that were "not far off" to see in the Christian gospel that which they really sought, and at the same time to combat the errors of those who were leading members of the church astray. The former would have been in mind as he wrote the Prologue, with the great confession of 1:14 ("the Word *became* flesh . . ."!) and its climax in 1:18. The same motive is discerned in his description of the death of Jesus and what happened when a soldier thrust a spear into the body of Jesus (19:32–35); his true humanity and real death were alike attested in that event. Those who stumble at Jesus and cause others to do so are mirrored in 6:60–69, a passage that finds an echo in 1 John 2:18–20; the corrections of the Gnostics in the Gospel are calculated to ensure that true believers do not follow their example.

More important than either of these two groups, attention is consistently paid to the Jews among whom Jesus ministered, with Jews of the synagogues of the evangelist's day in mind in particular. The opposition of Jewish leaders is highlighted throughout the Gospel. Indeed, the evangelist has an odd habit of speaking about "the Jews" when he really has in mind the Jewish opponents of Jesus, not the people (see e.g., 2:18, 20; 4:15, 16, 18; note the interchangeability of "the Jews" and "the Pharisees" in 9:13, 16, 18, 22; in the narrative "the Jews" primarily denote the Jewish leaders generally, as can be seen in 18:28-31, 38-40; 19:7, 12, 15). This would be more understandable if the evangelist had been a Gentile Christian, but there is no doubt that he was a Jew whose whole outlook is rooted in Judaism, and that he wrote in order that Jews and Gentiles should be converted. In 7:11, 12 he tells how "the Jews," i.e., the people who had come to Jerusalem to celebrate the Feast of Tabernacles, talked about Jesus, but did so quietly "for fear of 'the Jews'"! And many of "the Jews" believed in Jesus at that feast (7:31; 8:31)!

The notion that is gaining currency today, that the fourth Gospel is anti-Semitic, is quite mistaken. It is due to a failure to observe the various ways in which the author uses the term "the Jews," and also to not recognizing that the evangelist is at pains to show how the message and mission of Jesus is firmly set in the context of Israel's faith, hope, and promise. Quite certainly the frequent attention to the hostile Jewish leaders in this Gospel, the grounds of their opposition to Jesus, and his answers to them have in view the experience of the churches for which he wrote; history was being repeated, in that the hostility shown to Jesus was now being directed to his followers. They needed to understand their own situation and how to cope with it in light of what Jesus said and did when faced with similar opposition. Observe, moreover, that this concern of the evangelist was not solely from a negative point of view—i.e., to enable Christians to defend themselves against Jewish propaganda. He also wished to rectify the misunderstandings of his Jewish contemporaries. He wrote to help them see in Jesus the fulfillment of the revelation of God in the Old Testament and the fulfillment of the high points of their worship, especially as expressed in the great feasts of the Passover, Tabernacles, and Dedication. In short, he wrote to enable Jews to see in Jesus their Messiah, possessing a significance and stature greater even than the Old Testament had made known.

All this presupposes that the churches for which the evangelist wrote had among them a large proportion of Jews who were concerned to maintain their relationships with the synagogues. If the Gospel represents the witness of the beloved disciple it was probably formulated in Palestine, where most Christian congregations will have been entirely Jewish, and their members will have continued to worship in local synagogues as well as in their own Christian assemblies. Jewish Christians will have endeavored to continue these relationships even when, after the Jewish war with Rome, A.D. 66–70, they migrated to areas outside the Holy Land, notably to adjacent Syria and to Asia Minor. We learn from the Acts of the Apostles of the hostility experienced by young Christians in the entire Mediterranean area, not only of their expulsions from synagogues, but of accusations before Gentile authorities (cf. Acts 13:50; 14:1–7, 19; 17:4–9, 13; 18:12–17).

This situation became exacerbated rather than being diminished in the latter part of the first century. After the destruction of Jerusalem and its temple the Pharisees gained complete ascendancy over the Jewish people, and they reformulated Judaism in long consultations extending over many years in Jamnia. At some point in that period the deep opposition to Christians found expression in the Jewish daily prayers known as the Eighteen Benedictions, of which the twelfth was modified to read:

For apostates let there be no hope, and the dominion of arrogance [=Rome] do thou speedily root out in our days; and let the Nazarenes [=Christians] and heretics perish as in a moment, let them be blotted out of the

11   Interpreting the Gospel of John

book of the living and let them not be written with the righteous. Blessed art thou, O Lord, who humblest the arrogant.[3]

Whether that prayer had included the reference to the "Nazarenes" prior to the publication of our Gospel we have no means of knowing (we know *who* did it—Samuel the Small at the request of Rabbi Gamaliel, *Berakoth* 28b—but we do not know the *date* of its happening). That formulation of the prayer, however, brought to a head a long process of opposition to the Christian church, and above all, of course, to Jewish Christians. It illustrates the attitude which the latter had to endure in areas of Jewish domination. With all this in mind we read with quickened insight the controversies recorded in John 5, 7-9, the decision of the Sanhedrin to bring about the death of Jesus (11:45-54), and the warnings of Jesus in 15:18-16:4.

In pointing out this interest in the Jews we must not underestimate the importance of the world of nations to the evangelist. If the Jewish background of the gospel is unmistakable, the awareness of the outer world and concern for its peoples to learn of the only Savior of the world is equally evident. The Prologue relates the revelation of God in Christ to the whole creation and to the whole of humanity ("[*All*] that has come into being had its life in him, and the life was the light of men; . . . This was the authentic life, which enlightens *every* man by his coming into the world" 1:4, 9). The summary of the gospel in John 3:16, probably a confessional statement well known among the churches, makes it plain that the gospel is for every man, woman, and child in the world. So also the death and resurrection of Jesus has in view the redemption of *all* humankind, even as that dual event witnessed the exaltation of Jesus as Lord and Savior of the world (see especially 12:31, 32). The fourth Gospel makes it abundantly plain that the gospel proclaimed by Jesus, and which he is, takes into its scope the whole wide world, and there is no other Savior than he (4:42).

Jesus after the flesh —after the Spirit

We have left to the last what is perhaps the most important element in the interpretation of Jesus by the evangelist. The evangelist's desire to relate the story of Jesus to the situation of the churches in his day led him to an unusual procedure: *in his account of the works and words of Jesus he set the historical ministry of Jesus in Judea and Galilee in indissoluble relation to the ministry of the risen Lord in the world of his day.* The observation has been made by more than one writer that when Luke wrote an account of the origins of the Christian church he did it in two volumes: volume 1, the story of Jesus at work with his disciples among the Jews in Palestine; volume 2, the story of the risen Christ at work through his disciples among the nations of the world. By contrast the fourth evangelist wrote *one* book to cover both concerns, so that Jesus after the flesh and Jesus after the Spirit are presented together in a single perspective.

This brings with it the corollary that the relations of Jesus with his people during his ministry are continuous with the relations of the Lord with his church after Easter. The mission of Jesus to his people and the mission of the risen Lord to the world are one. In both he is the focal point of both faith and opposition in the world, and his disciples are inextricably bound up with Jesus in his destiny. With him they experience the powers of the kingdom of God which he brought, the opposition of the world to the preaching of his gospel, and also the positive response of many to that same gospel. This last feature happily is known by the disciples in greater measure than Jesus himself knew, in accordance with his own statement (14:12–14). This was the consequence of his dying and rising for the world's deliverance (12:31-32), and theirs was to be the privilege of reaping the harvest he had sown (12:23-24; cf. 4:37, 38).

J. Louis Martyn sought to illustrate what is involved in the presentation of Jesus in his ministry and Jesus after his resurrection by adducing the idea of a drama played out on a two-level stage, whereon the two sets of actors simultaneously work out a single plot. C. H. Dodd had already observed that the story of the Samaritan woman in chapter 4 is presented as a play in which one set of actors (Jesus, the disciples, the woman) is in the foreground and another group (the villagers, and the woman, who goes from one group to the other) stand at the back of the stage. Martyn saw in the narrative of the healing of the blind man in John 9 an ideal test case for his analogy: the first seven verses describe a typical "sign" performed by Jesus; the rest of the chapter tells what happens when a blind man's eyes are opened to God and the world, not alone by Jesus but by a Christian preacher, who did the same kind of thing in the name of Jesus. Martyn suggests that the two sections are not rigidly divided between past and present; rather, the whole narrative participates in the two-level drama.[4]

The analogy is not to be pressed, but it is not difficult to see in the experience of the blind man healed by Jesus, and the man's encounters with his neighbors, his parents, and the Pharisaic leaders. It is a picture of what many a Jew whose eyes were opened through the Light of the World (9:5) experienced in the time of the church. The story was doubtless written to enable this parallel to be grasped. The English commentator Sir Edwyn Hoskyns expressed the same kind of understanding as Martyn, but without the image of the two-story stage. Comparing the story of the healing of the paralytic at Bethesda in chapter 5 with that of the man born blind he wrote:

By a natural and unconscious symbolism the traditional narratives of his [Jesus'] miraculous actions were related in such a way as to identify the converts with those who had originally been healed, and the later opponents of Christianity with the original opponents of Jesus. The earlier narratives tended to become more and more clearly symbolical of the later experiences of the Christians, the original history providing the framework within which reference was made to contemporary history, and the materials out of which narratives and discourses could be constructed.[5]

This accords with the passage to which we have already drawn attention, John 14:12, 13: the works of Jesus in his ministry are to be continued by his disciples after his death, and *greater things* will be done by them, since Jesus will be with the Father. "Jesus with the Father," however, means not his absence, but his occupying the place of power and glory, so that when the disciples pray in his name *he* will act. They become the agents of the risen Lord for doing "greater things," for in the resurrection era and the presence of the Spirit *the spiritual realities signified by the "signs" become available to people.*

They may, for example, receive bread of life, not simply bread that perishes (ch 6), and the life of the eternal kingdom of God, of which recovery from sickness or even resurrection from the grave are but reflections. The narratives in which these things are described are like mirrors, in which the readers in John's day can see their own experiences of the Lord's dealings with them and the consequences of these events in the society of their day.

What we have pointed out with regard to the narratives of the Gospel applies also to the teaching. The French writer Xavier Léon-Dufour drew attention to the symbolism of

John in this connection. He pointed out that the presentation of Jesus to the world outside Palestine entailed a transition from the cultural setting in which Jesus lived to that of the churches in John's time and place. This involved changes in the significance of the symbolism in the different settings. For example, among the Jews bread is symbolic of heavenly food, and heavenly food is thought of in terms of the Law; among Christians (including Jewish-Christians) it becomes linked on another level with the bread and wine of the Lord's Supper.

These differing levels of symbolism are both discernible in chapter 6, the former in verses 30–33, the latter in 51–58; yet they are not confined to those verses nor are they to be viewed as belonging exclusively to two different eras. On the contrary, both are linked with the sign of the feeding of the multitude and are intertwined in the discourse. For this reason Léon-Dufour urges that as John sought to unite the past and the present of Jesus we should not *contrast* the two different interpretations but seek a *unified* one and try to discover the relationship between the present reality of the Spirit and the times past of Jesus among his people. This entails respecting the distinctiveness and the due significance of each context.

The teaching of Jesus recorded by the evangelist has to be related both to the setting of Jesus among the Jews of his time and to that of his followers in their time. "If we end up failing to recognize all this," said Léon-Dufour, "it is because we allow ourselves to be dazzled by the light of Easter." To do that could result in the obliteration of the roots of our faith in what took place once for all through Jesus in the time of Pontius Pilate in Israel. Accordingly we must take seriously that the evangelist in the Gospel has brought alive the past of Jesus by showing its relevance for the present. He has both projected the past of Jesus into the present and enabled the present to be understood in light of that past.

Reflection on this issue will lead us to recognize that the key to this insight of the evangelist is the doctrine of the Holy Spirit. He it is who teaches the disciples and calls to mind the words and works of Jesus. He acts as the agent of the risen Lord, preserving the memory of Jesus in the flesh and interpreting his words and deeds as he makes them live again in the experience of his people. This is not simply a case of reminding people of one who lived some time ago, and of making his words "live" through a vivid repetition of them. The Lord is *present* among his people, continuing to unfold his revelation through the Spirit. This is clearly stated in John 16:12–15:

> I have many things to say to you, but you cannot endure them now; but when he, the Spirit of truth, comes, he will guide you in the entire truth; he will not speak on his own authority, but he will speak all that he hears, and he will disclose to you the things that are coming.

The fullness of truth into which the Spirit guides, accordingly, is the word that Jesus earlier spoke and continues to speak as the risen Lord in an unbroken process of instruction. This the evangelist clearly understood. No wonder, then, that he could describe in the same breath what the Lord did and said in the days of his flesh and what he is doing and saying from the right hand of God. He was acting on the truth of what a contemporary of his said: "Jesus Christ is the same yesterday and today and for ever" (Hebrews 13:8 RSV)! In this witness to Christ, as F. Mussner pointed out, two time horizons merge, that of Jesus in Palestine and that of Jesus in glory. The incarnate Lord who acted and spoke in the power of the Spirit among his people speaks from heaven by the same Spirit to the evangelist. So it comes about that "the evangelist becomes the inspired mouthpiece of the glorified Christ; he lends him his tongue, so that the Christ speaks to the Christian community in John's very own language."[6]

To grasp this feature of the Gospel should lead the preacher, teacher, and church member who wishes to bear witness to the Lord to do the same, namely to lend his or her tongue to the risen Lord, and by the Spirit's aid to let him speak that revelation of his in the language of today.

For modern Western man, who has lost the key to the idiom of the Word, the Prologue to the fourth Gospel is an enigma. People of the nearer Orient and those of the Mediterranean area, who first contemplated this composition, will have been fascinated by it, and would have been lured on to read further about this unheard-of news of the Word *made flesh*.

Unlike the introductions to the other Gospels, the Prologue to John's Gospel is a complete composition. While written for the Gospel, it could conceivably be detached from it and serve as a catechetical statement as to who Jesus is. There is no evidence that it ever circulated on its own, but an increasing number of scholars believe that the Prologue was based on a hymn that was in use prior to the writing of the Gospel. It is noteworthy that the greatest affirmations in the New Testament letters as to the identity of Jesus and his deeds are expressed in hymns to the praise of Christ. I speak, of course, of notably Philippians 2:6–11, Colossians 1:15–20, 1 Timothy 3:16, to say nothing of the many snatches of hymns in the book of Revelation.

The poetic structure within the Prologue is clearest in verses 1-5, 10-12b, 14, 16, and 18. The statement about John the Baptist in verses 6-8 will have been inserted by the evangelist, probably because in his time there were followers of John who declared that *he* was the Light that brings salvation. The evangelist counters this by affirming that John was sent by God to be *a witness* to the one and only Light of the world. Verse 9 is uncertain; it would follow on verse 5 well, and closely link verses 1-5 to 10-12b; moreover, its thought of the Word as the light that illuminates every man continues that of verses 4-5.

On the other hand, the assertion that John the Baptist is not the Light, but was sent to bear witness to the Light, is well followed by the statement that the Word is the *authentic* Light that illuminates all humankind. We must acknowledge the uncertainty of the origin of the sentence. It is clear, however, that verse 16 follows directly on that of verse 14, that verse 15 is written in the same strain as verses 6-8, and that verse 17 provides comment on verse 16. The hymn of the Word of God may therefore have read as follows:

In the beginning was the Word,
and the Word was with God,
and the Word was God.
This was in the beginning with God.
Everything came into existence through him,
and apart from him not a thing came into being.
What has come into being had its life in him,
and the life was the light of men;
and the light shines on in the darkness,
and the darkness did not grasp it.
(This was the authentic light,
which enlightens every person by his coming into the
    world.)
He was in the world,

and the world came into existence through him,
and the world did not know him.
He came to his own domain
and his own people did not accept him.
But to all who did accept him,
he gave authority to become God's children.
And the Word became flesh,
and pitched his tent among us,
and we gazed on his glory,
glory such as belongs to the only Son from the Father,
full of grace and truth.
For a share of his fullness we all received,
even grace upon grace.
God no one has ever seen.
The only Son, by nature God, who is ever close to the
    Father's heart,
he has brought knowledge of him.

If it be asked why the evangelist utilized a hymn to introduce his Gospel the answer must be that it perfectly expressed his theology concerning Jesus. And indeed not simply his own, but that of the churches he served. It has been pointed out that while verses 1-5 and 10-12 are stated in the third person, verses 14 and 16 are in the first person plural—the language of confession. The idea has been mooted that verse 14 is a confessional response of believers to the utterances regarding the Word that have preceded, and that for a very important reason: the declarations concerning the Word in the earlier part of the poem were common in the ancient world, but Christians alone can affirm verse 14, with its affirmation of the incarnation of the Word.

This introduction to the gospel has been aptly likened to an overture to an opera. The function of an overture is to prepare the hearers for the musical drama that follows and, not infrequently, themes and songs which occur in the opera

        The Word Made Flesh

are anticipated in the overture. It is no accident that many motifs within the Prologue occur in the Gospel itself. Among such we may mention the preexistence of the Son of God (cf. 1:30; 17:5), his function as the Light of the world and its life (8:12; 11:25), the gift of the "only Son" in incarnation and in death for the world (3:16), the manifestation of his glory (2:11; 12:23; 13:31), the unbelief of the world in face of it (12:41; 16:8-11), the faith of those attracted by it (12:31, 32; 17:6-19), and most striking of all, the conclusion of the Gospel with the confession of Thomas, "My Lord and my God!" followed by the stated purpose of the Gospel that readers may come to a like faith in Jesus (20:28, 30, 31).

A. Loisy wrote, "The theology of the incarnation is the key of the entire book, and it dominates it from the first line to the last."[1] Not only did Sir Edwyn Hoskyns agree with that judgment; he went even further: "The figure of Jesus as the embodiment of the glory of the Word of God controls the whole matter of the Christian religion."[2]

"The Word" in ancient times

The opening phrase of the Prologue points to the fact that affirmations about the Word of God had been at home in the ancient world for a millennium and more: "*In the beginning was the Word* . . . ." We recall the first sentence of the Bible: "*In the beginning* God created . . . ." The association was inevitable for Jews, for they used to name the books of the Bible by their first word; Genesis, therefore, was known as "In the beginning." It was as if John wrote, "In that beginning of which Genesis speaks the Word was already there when God created the universe, and it was through him that God performed his creative works."

The thought, however, was equally familiar to Israel's neighbors, including the most distinguished of them, who in turn held sway over the Jews. The Assyrians and Babylonians in early times composed hymns about the Word of God, in which the Word appears as a quasiphysical power of cosmic proportions. It is described as "the exalted powerful Word . . . unfathomable and incomprehensible, closed up, mysterious." While the Word is compared with a raging storm or a bursting dam, or a net that catches all and from which none can escape, the hymns also speak of the Word's beneficent and life-giving activity in creation. In Egypt the Word was thought of as a heavenly divine substance, flowing out of the mouth of (the) god. Ptah was declared to be the creator of the world, and his instrument of creation was "the mouth which named all things," i.e., the Word.

Significantly in these ancient texts the creative Word is associated with Wisdom. Thoth, the Egyptian Hermes, is acknowledged to be the Word and the god of Wisdom. So also the Ras Shamra texts link the word and the wisdom of El (i.e., God): "Thy Word, O El, is wisdom; wise art thou eternally." That same connection is maintained in a whole series of texts in the Old Testament and early Jewish writings in their accounts of creation and God's maintenance of the universe.

In Proverbs 8:22–31 it is wisdom which was with God "from the beginning, before the world began," and was present as "the craftsman at his side" when creation was formed. The Book of Wisdom 9:1, 2 sets Word and Wisdom in parallelism in the work of creation:

> O God of our Fathers . . .
> who made all things by your Word
> and by your Wisdom formed man . . .

Yet more remarkably, Word and Wisdom became linked with the Law (Torah, as the Jews called it). In the Wisdom of Jesus Ben Sira (*Ecclesiasticus*) a description of Wisdom concludes with the words, "All this is the covenant book of the Most High, *the Law* which Moses enacted to be the heritage of the assemblies of Jacob." This identification of Law with Wisdom led to the (to us!) extraordinary notion that the Law was God's means of creation. The expression "in the beginning" in Hebrew is a single word, and it can as well be rendered, "by the beginning." One rabbinic commentator, favoring the latter meaning, drew the conclusion: "The beginning is nothing other than the Torah," citing as evidence Proverbs 8:22. Hence Genesis 1:1 means that the Law was God's instrument in the creation of all things. So, in Judaism Word, Wisdom, and Law became interchangeable terms.

From the ancient nearer Orient the concept of the Word passed into the learning of Greece and Rome. Augustine, in a famous passage of his Confessions, related how he procured "certain books of the Platonists" and read in them most of what is stated of the Word in the Prologue. But there were others besides the "Platonists" who so wrote of the Word (the Logos). Heraclitus in the sixth century B.C. described the Word as "the omnipresent wisdom by which all things are guided"; he identified it with the word of God received by the prophets and regarded the Word as virtually an equivalent for God. The Stoics regarded the Word as the common law of nature, the soul of the universe, maintaining its unity. Philo, the Jew of Alexandria, a contemporary of Jesus who sought to mediate the Jewish faith to the literary world of his day, wrote much about the Word. He spoke of the Word as the agent of creation and the medium of God's government of the world. It is the Mediator, the High Priest through whom the world comes to God, and even the Advocate (Paraclete) for the forgiveness of sins. He stated that for the mass of people God is unknowable, but the ordinary folk can know him in and through the Word. The Word is the perfect Man, the Man of Genesis 1, made in the image of God, as distinct from the man of Genesis 2, made of the dust of the earth. He is the Father's "eldest Son," his "Firstborn." There is no ground for believing that Philo's writings were known at first hand to the fourth evangelist; the two writers rather reflect the common thinking that was in circulation in their day.

The same has to be said of the similarities between John's writing and the works of the Gnostics. In the dualistic thought of this widespread movement the Word was the Mediator between God and the world. Through him the transcendent God was able to create this lower material world, and because of him men and women may understand that they belong to God and *his* world. So the Gnostics viewed the Word as the Redeemer who came in human form into the lower world to lead humankind back into the higher world of God. They called him the "second God," the Son of God, the Only Son, the Image of God, the Man.

Christ — the Word

This brief review suffices to show that the Word of God was an ancient and international concept, with connotations buried deep in the cultures of the Eastern and Western world. There was, however, one factor in the use of this term that decisively modified its meaning for Christians: they commonly used it to denote the gospel of Christ, that is, the Word of God spoken *through* Christ and *about* Christ. Once it was grasped that the Word of God for the world is Christ, the incarnate, crucified, and exalted Lord, the employment of the term "the Word" as an inclusive, descriptive title was inevitable; and in turn that invested the term with a unique meaning, and made possible a bridge to the religions and philosophies of the ancient world. T. Boman suggested that the effect produced by the use of "the Word" in the Prologue should be compared with the ringing of many bells in people's hearing (see his exposition, *Hebrew Thought Compared with Greek*, 58–69).[3] Certainly no statement in the Prologue would have roused the interest of

The Word Made Flesh

pagan readers more than the astonishing assertion, "And the Word *became flesh.*"

This leads to an interesting question: in light of the movement of the Prologue from the activity of the Word in Creation to the announcement of the Word made flesh, at what point in the passage do we begin to read of the work of the *earthly* Christ? There is difference of opinion about this. Some see Jesus in his ministry as early as verses 4 and 5; others put the transition at verse 9; in either case the confessional statement of verse 14 summarizes the revelation of the Word in the historical Jesus just described, as though the evangelist meant "*and so* the Word became flesh . . . ."

An important question immediately arises. The Christian, indeed, can hardly avoid seeing in verses 10–12 a reference to the rejection of Jesus by the majority of his own people and the acceptance of the gospel in the wider world, and similarly in verse 13 the ministry of the Spirit after Pentecost. Nevertheless, there can be no doubt that the *entire* description of verses 1–13 would have made perfect sense to non-Christian people of all nationalities who knew about the Word. They acknowledged the Word as God's means of creation, as the source of life, and the light of all humankind, not least in view of the relation of Word and Wisdom. Such people were aware of the darkness of this world, the ignorance among many of the Word and its Wisdom, and even hostility to and rejection of the Light. There is a persistent strain in the ancient poetry of Wisdom that depicts her as descending from heaven to find a place of welcome on earth, but unable to find any. Enoch 42:2 is a late example of this:

> Wisdom went forth to make her dwelling among the
> children of men,
> and found no dwelling place;
> Wisdom returned to her place,
> and took her seat among the angels.

Whereas Jews typically maintained that they, and they alone, made a home for Wisdom, i.e., in the Law given them by God (Ben Sira 24:6-8), the evangelist implies that people of other nations made a place for the Word in their lives, to whom also God graciously ministered. In this he was not alone among members of his race who pondered the issue. In the book entitled The Wisdom of Solomon, chapter 7, there is an unusual description of Wisdom, clearly akin to Greek thinking, wherein the following occurs:

> She is the brightness that streams from everlasting light, the flawless mirror of the active power of God and the image of his goodness. She is but one, yet can do everything; herself unchanging, she makes all things new; age after age she enters into holy souls, and makes them God's friends and prophets, for nothing is acceptable to God but the man who makes his home with wisdom . . . . She spans the world in power from end to end, and orders all things benignly (7:26-8:1).

This activity of Wisdom assuredly is not confined within Israel's borders! So also the Prologue is consciously worded with a view to taking into account the universal ministry of the Word in the world, who is not alone the source of all life but also the source of the world's "light" (it is "the authentic light that enlightens *every* person," v 9). This life and light has been operative among humankind from the dawn of time, with varied responses from people (vv 10–12), until at length the ministry of the Word came to its climax in a ministry in the flesh. Since the Word is always the same in character, it is assumed that his service in the flesh was conducted in the same manner as that in the ages prior to his incarnation. However, in the earthly ministry the grace and truth of the Word was unambiguously *revealed* so that what was partially known came to be luminously plain.

C. H. Dodd accordingly suggested that the whole passage from verse 4 is at once "an account of the relations of the *Logos* (the Word) with the world, *and* an account of the ministry of Jesus Christ, which in every essential particular reproduces those relations."[4] This is especially clear with regard to verses 4-13, with which we were concerned; the description of the activity of the Word in that passage holds good both of the preincarnate and the incarnate Word, even if the language is more especially suitable to the latter. From this understanding of the Prologue Dodd advanced to a further conclusion regarding the relation of the Prologue to the whole Gospel. He stated:

> We might put it thus: the Prologue is an account of the life of Jesus under the form of a description of the eternal *Logos* (Word) in its relations with the world and with man, and the rest of the gospel an account of the *Logos* (Word) under the form of a record of the life of Jesus. And the proposition 'the Word became flesh' binds the two together.[5]

That is profound insight into the nature of the Gospel and its presentation of Jesus, and I believe it to be a right interpretation.

Christ—the Mediator

It is evident that the dominant concept of the Word in the Prologue is that of Mediator: he is Mediator in creation (vv 1-4a, 10), in revelation (vv 4b, 5, 18), and in salvation (vv 12, 13, 16). The opening statement makes plain the ground on which the Word can fulfill such a role by defining his relation to God. The evangelist has very carefully chosen his words, and we must as carefully consider them.

The Word was "in the beginning." Note the difference between "was" in this clause and "came to be" in verse 3, used in relation to the creation of the world. The latter statement declares that all things "came into existence" through him, whereas the force of verse 1 is that "in the beginning *he was there,* with God," or even, as some render it, "he *always was* with God." The intent of the opening statement is to make clear the existence of the Word before all time. Bultmann rightly observed, "The beginning is not the first member of a temporal succession, but lies before all time and therefore before all worlds."[6] In that unimaginable eternity before all time the Word was "with God." That is, he was "in the fellowship of God" (cf. 17:5, and 1 John 1:2, 3). The expression conveys the thought of the ineffable union of the Word with God, which later in the Gospel is spoken of in terms of mutual indwelling of the Father and the Son (cf. 14:10).

The final clause of this opening sentence runs, "and the Word was God." He was "with God" and "was God"—at once distinction and identification! But is identification really meant? It is well known that whereas in the preceding clause the evangelist writes, "the Word was with God" (Greek *ho theos,* with the defining definite article), in this succeeding clause he writes, "and the Word was *theos,* " without the definite article. A difference of expression is being made, but with what intent? Not, assuredly, in order to say, "the Word was *a god,* " as the Jehovah's Witnesses maintain, citing certain Christian scholars in support (including J. Becker, author of the most recent German commentary on the Gospel at the time of writing this work). Becker, of course, is aware that the evangelist is using an earlier hymn to the Word, and he proceeds on the assumption that the language is originally that of a pre-Christian author.

We have already seen that the hymn expresses an understanding of the Word widespread in the ancient world. No

The Word Made Flesh

doubt religious devotees of ancient Egypt, Assyria, Babylonia, and more recent Greece and Rome could have confessed their faith in the Word as "a god," but not Christian believers in the *one* God of the Bible, least of all the evangelist who wrote this sentence. He is showing how this ancient faith in the Word of God comes to its true fulfillment in the Son of God, incarnate in Jesus. It is admittedly conceivable that the evangelist wished to say that Jesus was *divine,* using *theos* as a kind of adjective. But there is an adjective in Greek that means precisely that, *theios,* which occurs twice in 2 Peter 1—of the "divine power" (v 3) and of the "divine nature" (v 4). If that is what was in the evangelist's mind he could have said so plainly.

In reality what was in his mind is likely to have been in that direction, but more emphatic: "The Word was *theos*" means "the Word was *God in his nature.*" That is in harmony with the thought of the Word as Mediator of creation, of revelation, and of salvation, who before all time was in the fellowship of God, and therefore one with God. It is noteworthy that in the confession made by Thomas to Jesus (20:28) there is no limitation in expressing the unity of Jesus with God as he cries, "My Lord and *my God!*" (in Greek *ho kurios mou kai ho theos mou*). This understanding of John 1:1c is well conveyed by the NEB: "what God was, the Word was."

After the reaffirmation of the truth of verse 1 in verse 2, the function of the Word in the world as the life and the light of all humanity is declared. In view of the dual relation of verses 4–13 to the Word before and after his incarnation in Jesus, we are to understand the bestowal of life and light in verses 4 and 5 as including the life and light which come to man in both creation and new creation (viewing new birth in 3:3–8 as participating by the Spirit in the new creation). The same dual application holds good of verses 9–13, although verses 12c and 13 are peculiarly expressive of the Christian experience of regeneration by the Spirit.

All the affirmations of the Prologue from its beginning to verse 13 move to the climactic utterance in verse 14: "The Word became flesh." To all who shared the traditions of the ancient Oriental world about the Word the statement is all but incredible. If it had said that the Word descended from heaven to live within a human body for a while, that would have still been surprising, but at least it would have been comprehensible—stories of the gods visiting the world in human likeness were not uncommon (cf. Acts 14:11!). And for any who looked on this sphere as a lower world, unworthy of the divine, God and flesh are antitheses that can never be united. But that is precisely what is here affirmed: The unbridgeable gulf was crossed, and the Word *became* flesh! The assertion banishes any shade of Docetism from authentic Christian faith. The Word of God became a *real* man, not a *seeming* one!

And so the Word "pitched his tent" among us (Greek *eskenosen*, forming the noun *skene*, a tent). The old English term "tabernacled" points to what is in mind, namely the presence of God with his people in the wilderness wanderings of the Exodus. The pillar of cloud by day and of fire by night, which guided the Jews from Egypt to the promised land (Exod 13:21, 22), was a sign of the presence of God with his people; it rested on the "tent of meeting" (Exod 33:7–11), and at the consecration of the tabernacle it filled it with its glory (Exod 40:34–38).

The Jews noticed that the Greek term for tent, *skene*, had the same consonants as the Hebrew *šekina*, the presence of God which often manifested itself among men in a show of glory. It was actually said by one Jewish teacher that the consecration of the tabernacle was the first day of the Shekinah's existence in the universe—a pardonable exaggeration which nevertheless indicates the special connection between the glorious presence of God in the midst of his people and the tabernacle during the wilderness wanderings.

Accordingly the statement in verse 14, "he pitched his tent among us and we gazed on his glory," is deeply evocative. On the one hand it recalls the revelation of God's presence with his people in the Exodus, and on the other it points to the fulfillment of the Jewish hope of a second Exodus, when God would deliver his people through the "second Redeemer" (Moses being the first) for the salvation of the kingdom of God (cf. Jer 31:31-33; Ezek 20:33-44; Hos 2:14-23).

When the Word "pitched his tent" and revealed his glory, the process of redemption began. The glory became visible in his total activity—in the "signs" of his ministry (cf. 2:11), in his "lifting up" on the cross (12:23; cf. 19:35, 36), and in the Easter resurrection (20:24-29). It was a glory such as could be revealed solely in "the only Son from the Father," i.e., in God's only Son.

The term translated "only" (*monogenes*) means literally "the only one (*monos*) of its kind (*genos*)." In the Greek Bible, it often is used to render the Hebrew word *yahid*, used of an "only" or "beloved" child; but *yahid* is also translated by the term *agapetos*, "beloved." A clear example of the meaning of the word is seen in Judg 11:34: Jephthah's daughter is said to be "his only child (*yahid*); beside her he had neither son nor daughter." The Greek Bible translates *yahid* in that passage in a twofold manner, *monogenes . . . agapetos*, i.e., "his *only* and *beloved* child."

In Gen 22, where Isaac is three times stated to be Abraham's *yahid* (vv 2, 12, 16) the Greek Bible uses *agapetos*, "beloved" child; interestingly, Heb 11:17 when citing this story, uses *monogenes*, "only," with reference to Isaac!

It is evident that in our Gospel *monogenes*, which is used solely of Jesus, has the simple meaning of God's *only* Son. The additional term "begotten," which some still wish to use, is not contained in the word itself. If, as some think, there is in verse 14 any reminiscence of the term in 1:13, "begotten of God" (a quite different word) the parallel would be to the begetting of Jesus *as a man*, without human father, not to the generation of the Son from the Father. But verse 14 is likely to have been formed as an independent confessional statement, and therefore is to be understood without reference to verse 13.

The glory of the Word-become-flesh was "full of grace and truth"—the latter is a pregnant and significant phrase, for it represents a frequent expression in the Old Testament to describe the covenant mercies of God.

A good example occurs in the revelation of the glory of God to Moses, when the name of God is proclaimed, concluding with the description "abounding in steadfast love and faithfulness" (RSV). Surprisingly, perhaps, the term "grace" occurs only in this paragraph in the fourth Gospel (vv 14–17), but the emphatic nature of these statements shows their importance to the evangelist. He is here confessing, with the whole church of God, the nature of the glory of God manifest in Jesus the incarnate Word: It is full of the steadfast love that pours itself out on the needy and undeserving. The point is underlined in verse 16: from him we have received "grace upon grace," i.e., inexhaustible grace, replacing grace received by fresh grace bestowed, *ad infinitum!* "Truth," in the context of the covenant faithfulness of God in the Old Testament, represents firmness and stability, therefore steadfastness and trustworthiness regarding the promises of God. Such commitment of God to his covenant love reaches its perfect expression in the "tabernacling" of his only Son among men in order to bring to pass the reiterated promise of salvation. When the Word became flesh the kingdom of grace and glory among mankind was assured. "We gazed on his glory . . . full of grace and truth" is the testimony of those who *saw* it in action in the world.

The final statement of the Prologue echoes its opening utterance. Unfortunately we cannot be sure of the original wording of the second clause. Either we are to read "the only Son (by nature) God" (*monogenes theos*) or "the only Son of God" (*monogenes huios*); the earliest manuscripts of the Gospel support the former, many others the latter reading. Most textual critics accept the former reading on the ground of the superior authority of manuscripts and its greater difficulty. In addition, this reading makes the link with the first sentence of the Prologue more evident. The last clause of verse 1, "the Word was God," we interpreted as "the Word was *God in his nature*"; that is almost verbally the same as our rendering of verse 18b, "the only Son, *by nature God.*" The only Son is said to be "ever close to the Father's heart" (literally "in the bosom of the Father"); that is a more picturesque and emphatic way of saying, "the Word was *with God,*" which we interpreted as "in the fellowship of God."

The fundamental thought of verse 18, accordingly, is the same as that of verse 1, but it has a particular nuance, in that it is concerned with the revelation brought by the Word. A contrast is being made with claims to revelations of God made by other religious leaders. "Nobody has ever seen God" includes all visionaries of all religions, including those of Israel. Manifestly it does not affirm that no one has ever caught a *glimpse* of God, not when the writer is a Jew who knows his Old Testament! Curiously, however, it is almost certain that the man whom the Jews regarded as the closest to God in all time is consciously included in the affirmation, namely Moses. The evangelist has already referred to him in the previous sentence; as he pens verse 18 from an earlier composition he could not help thinking about Moses. Exod 33:18ff. tells how Moses asked to see the glory of God. This was denied him, since "man shall not see God and live." But he was put in a cleft of the rock as the Lord passed by, the hand of God covering his face, and Moses was allowed to see God's *back*. That, and no more! And from that partial vision of God proceeded the Law, in the eyes of the Jew the most sacred part of the revelation of God in the Old Testament.

By contrast, the only Son, by nature God, is "close to the Father's heart." The primary reference is to his fellowship with the Father in his incarnate life; but it includes the relation to the Father of the preincarnate existence of the Word, and also that which he continues to know in his post-Easter existence (17:5). Accordingly the "exposition" of God that he has given in the flesh, and ratified in the resurrection, is superior to all declarations of God in time and is to be viewed as a "final" revelation.

We observed earlier that the theology of the Prologue is the key to the entire Gospel. That was primarily intended with regard to the presentation and interpretation of Jesus in the Gospel.

It is noteworthy that in the crucial statement as to the Incarnation of the Word, the glory revealed in him is described as "such as belongs to *the only Son from the Father.*" The glory of the Word was the glory of the only Son. So also the conclusion of the Prologue affirms that the ultimate revelation of the Father has been given through "the only Son, by nature God." The Son, like the Word, discloses God because he is one with God. That theme runs through the Gospel to its conclusion. The conclusion rams it home (20:24–31)! Whereas, however, the Word as a title does not appear after the Prologue, "the Son" (or "Son of God") is the most characteristic term for Jesus in the Gospel.

One of the interesting features of recent biblical studies is awareness of the importance of the concept "Son of God" within Israel. Most commonly it was applied to the nation in its relation to God as his adopted son (in Exod 4:22, 23 Israel is referred to as God's firstborn son, in contrast to Pharaoh's

The Word Made Flesh

firstborn). In 2 Sam 7:14 it is made known to David that his descendants will be as God's son. The thought is developed in Ps 2:7 and 89:26, 27; the king on the day of his coronation becomes God's adopted son. Naturally this led to the thought of the Messiah as son of God in virtue of his representative capacity, and his function as God's king, an idea developed by the Qumran sectaries. We see this reflected in the high priest's question to Jesus at his trial: "Are you the Messiah, *the Son of the Blessed One?*" That is a typical Jewish mode of expression, with its avoidance of the name of God and the title Son of God as designating the Messiah.

It is important to observe that this level of meaning given to "Son of God" appears in the account of the disciples' earliest reactions to Jesus in the fourth Gospel. They are introduced within the circle of John the Baptist's followers. They hear John's testimony to Jesus, "Look, there is *the Lamb of God!*" (That title is an apocalyptic designation for the Messiah, which we shall consider later in our reflections on the death of Jesus.) It prompts Andrew and another disciple to spend a night with Jesus; on return he tells his brother, "We have found *the Messiah!*" Nathanael, on being brought to Jesus by Philip, is overcome by the knowledge Jesus displays of him and he cries, "Rabbi, you are *the Son of God*, you are *the King of Israel!*" In this setting these titles ascribed to Jesus are synonymous. The Gospel will show the development of the disciples' comprehension of Jesus and the deeper significance that these terms receive through their application to Jesus.

A stage in that development of understanding is recorded in the evangelist's account of the aftermath of the feeding of the multitude, John 6. The excitement generated by that event led a crowd to try to compel Jesus to become king (6:14, 15); their enthusiasm melted away on hearing Jesus expound his mission in terms of giving bread of life to the world, and many of his adherents left him on that day (6:60–66). When Jesus asked the Twelve if they, too, wished to go off Peter replied, "Lord, to whom are we to go? You have words of eternal life. And we have come to believe and to know that you are the Holy One of God" (6:68, 69). There is no alternative to Jesus! The apostle's answer reveals that the early enthusiastic expressions of faith have given place to more mature belief and a deeper knowledge of Jesus. They have come to see in Jesus "the Holy One of God."

In this context the expression is likely to be a synonym for Messiah. There is a closely parallel statement of Jesus himself in 10:36, where he makes reference to his being "consecrated and sent into the world," i.e., to bring to humankind the saving sovereignty of God. But the expression inevitably recalls the common name for God in the Old Testament, "the Holy One of Israel." The implication of the title is that Jesus shares the holiness and therefore the nature of him whom Israel confesses as *the* Holy One. That comports with the word of Jesus already cited, that the Father has *consecrated and sent him into the world* for his service. There is accordingly ground for Bultmann's comment on Peter's confession of Jesus: "He stands over against the world simply as the One who comes from that other world and belongs to God."[7]

This brings us back to the connection between the Son and the Word in the Prologue. There we see the "only Son" (*monogenes*) as one with the Father in the eternal ages, sent by the Father to *reveal* him (v 18) and to *redeem* mankind (v 14). These concepts appear again and again in the body of the Gospel. In the famous text, John 3:16: "God so loved the world that he *gave* his only Son . . . " the giving of the Son includes giving for incarnation and giving in death for the life of the world. The immediately following sentence (3:17) comprehends both ideas in the simple word "sent": "For God did not send the Son into the world in order to condemn the world, but that the world might be saved through him." John 3:18 contemplates the effects of the mission of the Son in salvation and condemnation, according to the response of people; and in 3:19 these issues are expressed in language used of the Word of God in the Prologue (1:5, 9-12).

The paragraph 3:31-36 gives another meditation on the sending of the Son in similar vein as 3:16-21, only the accent in this passage falls on the task of the Son to *reveal* God. This is seen especially in verses 31-34. On the one hand the Son bears testimony to what he has seen and heard (v 32), which includes seeing and hearing in his preincarnate state and in his continuing ministry among his people; on the other hand the Father has given to the Son the Spirit "without measure." Rabbi Aha stated:

> The Holy Spirit who rests on the prophets rests on them only by measure [i.e., in a limited fashion,] (*Lev. Rab.* 15, 2).

To the immeasurable gift of the Spirit to the Son of God corresponds the perfection of the revelation through him. The paragraph ends with the assertion that the Father has placed "all things" in the hands of the Son, hence the ultimate issues of salvation and judgment are bound up with faith in him or rejection of him. The theme is further developed in 5:20-29.

Just as there is a link between the Son and the Word of God in the Gospel, so there is an even closer link between the Son (of God) and the Son of Man. The depiction in Daniel 7 of one like a son of man, coming with the clouds of heaven to receive the kingdom of God and rule over it, is determinative for the use of the title in the synoptic Gospels; in the earthly ministry of Jesus as the Son of Man, in his dying and rising and in his coming in glory, he is the instrument of the kingdom of God. Something similar appears in the fourth Gospel.

The first statement concerning the Son of Man in this Gospel provides a comprehensive preview of his mediatorial work. "You will see heaven standing open, and the angels of God going up and coming down to the Son of Man" (v 51). There is here a reminiscence of Jacob's dream, wherein angels ascend and descend on a ladder between heaven and earth. The implication is clear: Jesus is the point of contact between heaven and earth; this the disciples will see through his whole ministry—in the signs he performs, the word he utters, the life that he lives, the death and resurrection that he accomplishes, till the goal of his labors is attained when he welcomes the redeemed to the Father's house (14:3). This affirmation is a summary of the service of the Son of Man for the achievement of God's saving purpose for humankind.

But we have just seen that the salvation of humankind is the intention of the sending of the Son of God! This points to an interpenetration of the works of the Son of God and the Son of Man in the fourth Gospel, of which there are numerous examples. The classic statement of the purpose of the "giving" of the only Son of God in 3:16 is immediately preceded by the first of the three "lifting up" sayings of the Gospel, viz. 3:14, 15:

As Moses lifted up the snake in the desert, so the Son of Man must be lifted up, in order that everyone who believes may have in him eternal life" (cf. also 8:28; 12:31–32).

It is the task of the Son of Man to mediate the kingdom of God to the world.

In the discourse of 5:19–29, however, this task is delivered to *the Son* by the Father: "The Father loves the Son, and shows him everything that he himself does" (v 20). So he gives to the Son the power to raise the dead and to exercise judgment. Later on, however, it is affirmed, "He gave him authority to pass judgment, *because he is Son of Man*" (v 27)! A clearer example of the identity of functions of Jesus as Son of God and Son of Man could not be contrived. In reality the works of the Son of God who is Son of Man are ultimately the works of God through him. Accordingly his unity with the Father is emphasized: in terms of the Son in 10:30 ("I and the Father are One," cf. 10:29), and in terms of the Son of Man in 8:28 ("When you lift up the Son of Man, then you will know that '*I am*' . . . ").

The "I am" sayings

This last utterance naturally leads to a brief consideration of what are commonly known as the "I am" sayings of Jesus in the fourth Gospel. The seven sayings in which Jesus speaks of himself in various figurative ways, introduced by "I am," are among the best known passages of the Gospel. They cry out to be preached on! They are, in order of appearance, "I am the bread of life" (6:35; cf. 41, 48, 51); "I am the Light of the world" (8:12, cf. 9:5); "I am the Door (or *Gate* of the sheep)" (10:7, 9); "I am the Good Shepherd" (10:11, 14); "I am the resurrection and the life" (11:25); "I am the Way, the Truth, and the life" (14:6); "I am the Vine" (15:1, 5). These affirmations set forth what Jesus is for the world, though in practice it is believers who understand these realities as they experience them. The various images describe differing aspects of his saving work, more explicitly the life of the divine sovereignty (the kingdom of God) which Jesus brings to the world. Since Jesus possesses the life-giving power of the Father (5:21) Raymond Brown is right in observing, "Jesus is these things to men because he and the Father are One."[8]

There is another group of sayings in which "I am" is used absolutely. Certain of these serve to identify Jesus, as in 6:20, when Jesus comes to his disciples on the water and says to them, "I am (he), don't be afraid." Almost certainly we are intended in this passage to recall the coming of God to the Israelites in their peril at the Red Sea (see Psalm 77:14-20). Similarly, when Jesus declared to the soldiers who came to arrest him in the garden, "I am (he)," his simple self-identification created an element of divine dread, inasmuch as at least certain of the soldiers fell to the ground in confusion (18:5, 6). The other instances of the absolute use of the expression "I am" are yet more striking (8:20, 24, 58; 13:19); they recall the unique name of God made known to Moses in the vision at the burning bush (Exod 3:14) and certain affirmations of God in the central chapters of the book of Isaiah, notably in 43:10-13, 25; 45:5, 6, 18, 21, 22. The first of these passages is especially instructive:

> "You are my witnesses," says the Lord,
> "and my servant whom I have chosen,
> that you may know and believe me
> and understand that I am He.
> Before me no god was formed,
> nor shall there be any after me.
> I, I am the Lord,
> and besides me there is no savior.
> I declared and saved and proclaimed
> when there was no strange god among you;
> and you are my witnesses," says the Lord.
> "I am God, and also henceforth I am He;
> there is none who can deliver from my hand;
> I work and who can hinder me?" (RSV)

In the first sentence of this citation the phrase "I am He" has in Hebrew no verb; literally, it is simply "I . . . He" (the Hebrew mind supplies the verb "am"). In the Greek translation of the Old Testament this is rendered simply "I am" (*ego eimi*), and that is what our evangelist consistently writes. But in Isa 43:10 "I (am) He" is an abbreviation of "I, I am He, the Lord" of the following verse 11. There is indeed evidence that among the Jews "I (am) He" can appear as a substitute for "I am the Lord." Later in the same chapter, v 25, the language is again noteworthy: "I, I am He who blots out your transgressions"; in the Greek translation that appears, "I am 'I AM,' who blots out your transgressions." The second "I am" is viewed as a reminiscence of the name of God revealed at the Exodus and so understood as a title.

These associations of the expression "I am" were current in the first century of our era, and were developed even further by the rabbis (on these developments see the interesting discussion in C. H. Dodd's *The Interpretation of the Fourth Gospel*, pp 93–96). Their appropriation by and for Jesus suggests not so much a direct self-identification of Jesus with God as a union with God, by virtue of which God speaks and acts through Jesus as his representative and mediator of salvation and judgment.

We add one final reflection on Jesus in the Gospel of John: time and again it is made clear by the evangelist that the relation of Jesus to God becomes the great issue before which people divide (e.g., 7:43; 9:16; 10:19, and cf. 3:18–21; 12:31, 32). Perhaps we should not be surprised that this is most evident in the passage wherein Jesus uses the absolute "I am" most frequently and most challengingly (8:20, 24, 58). Whereas there were those who were drawn to faith in Jesus then (v 30), the implicit claims in the expression evoked the most violent hostility possible (v 59). The twofold perspective of the Gospel reminds us that precisely the same reactions occurred in the period when the Gospel was written; the decision for or against Jesus as the Son of God—Son of Man—Word of God became the ultimate cause of the separation of the church and synagogue. It remains so to this day, but extends beyond the Jewish people to the religions and ideologies of this world. Jesus is the touchstone of the revelation of God and his redemption of humankind. Before this issue all men and women are called to the bar of decision. It is not solved simply by verbal agreement or disagreement with Jesus but by willingness to be committed to the God revealed in him. It is the task of the church so to make him known that the truth of the revelation and the power of the redemption become luminously clear—not a stumbling-block, but the Way, the Truth, and the Life.

3   THE SIGNS OF JESUS AND THEIR SIGNIFICANCE

It is well known that seven "signs" of Jesus are recounted in the Gospel of John—quite certainly a number deliberately chosen, seven being associated by the Jews with perfection. In the synoptic Gospels the evangelists do not describe the miracles of Jesus as "signs"; they use rather the ordinary Greek term for miracle, namely *dynamis* (cf. dynamic, dynamite). That term normally means "power," but it can also have a concrete sense, a "powerful deed." Conversely the term *dynamis* does not occur in any sense in the Gospel and Letters of John.

The term "sign" has a long history among the Jewish people. In the Old Testament it is frequently used of events, both natural and supernatural, that authenticate the ministry and the message of a prophet. The signs announced by Samuel to Saul confirming the genuineness of his message from God that Saul is to be king, is an interesting example of natural events serving as signs (1 Sam 10:1-9); the supernatural actions that Moses is told to perform before the Jewish elders illustrate the latter kind of signs (Exod 4:1-8,

29-31). The judgments of the Lord on Egypt, performed at the word of Moses, are regularly referred to as "signs and wonders" (Exod 7:13 by anticipation, Deut 6:22 retrospectively). In Jer 32:20 the whole series of Exodus events, from the departure from Egypt to the entry into the promised land, are spoken of as signs and wonders, and these are said to be continued by God throughout the earth "to this day." Psalm 136 brackets those same events with the wonders of God's actions in creation.

An important application of "signs and wonders" is the expectation of their taking place to herald the future, especially the final future of the kingdom of God. An early example of this is seen in Isa 7:10-16, but it becomes highly developed in later apocalyptic writings.

The Gospels are at one in the application of this teaching to Jesus: nothing less than signs of the kingdom of God are at work in this world in and through Jesus. This understanding of the signs is clearly set forth in Matt 11:5, 6, 12, 13; 12:28; 13:16, 17; Mark 3:27; Luke 4:16-21; 17:20, 21. The fourth evangelist both clarifies and emphasizes this interpretation. He sees the miracles as parables of the kingdom that comes through the work of the Son of God. The signs of Jesus are powerful manifestations of the kingdom in the earthly ministry of Jesus, but they are also anticipations of the "greater things" (14:12) of the kingdom that comes yet more decisively in his own greater works—in his death and resurrection, the sending of the Holy Spirit, and the final coming of the Lord for last judgment and resurrection. As in the Old Testament the coming of God for his kingdom results in the gathering of the Gentiles to see his glory, (Isa 66:19), so the signs of Jesus are revelations of *his* glory. The kingdom that comes through the Son is the kingdom of God in Christ. Of this the signs of Jesus are revelations.

The manner in which the signs of Jesus are presented by our evangelist is of particular interest. They dominate the story of the public ministry of Jesus, so much so that C. H. Dodd called chapters 2–12 of the Gospel "The Book of Signs." The general procedure of the evangelist is to relate a sign, or two signs, and to follow on with teaching that explains the significance of the sign(s). On one occasion a miraculous sign is combined with a nonmiraculous event, each contributing to an exposition of the gospel of considerable length (see chapter 2, which describes the miracle of the Water into Wine and the Cleansing of the Temple; the former prepares for the Nicodemus discourse in chapter 3, the latter for the exposition of the new order of worship in chapter 4).

There is even one instance of two nonmiraculous signs being followed by an explanatory discourse, exactly as the miraculous signs are followed by like instruction (ch 12, the anointing of Jesus by Mary and the Entry into Jerusalem, seen as signs of the burial of Jesus and his exaltation). It was Dodd's merit to have perceived that in each episode of signs plus discourse the gospel in its wholeness is presented, the good news of Christ manifest, crucified, risen, exalted, and bestowing life.[1] It seems evident that the evangelist himself will have used these episodes time and again in his own proclamation and teaching of the gospel. His procedure is an invitation to modern witnesses to Christ to use them in precisely the same way.

It is now our task to review briefly the accounts of the signs of Jesus in the Gospel and consider the lessons that we are intended to learn from them.

The water into wine

The first miraculous sign, that of the Water into Wine, is bound up with a highly important nonmiraculous action of Jesus, namely the Cleansing of the Temple. We are certainly intended to perceive a relation between the two events, as is indicated by the evangelist's placing the cleansing at the beginning of the ministry instead of at its end, and even more because the discourses that follow are integrally connected with the two signs (ch 3 with the Water into Wine, ch 4 with the Temple of the Living Lord). It is highly unlikely that in setting the account of the temple cleansing at this point in the narrative the evangelist wishes to show that it is a different event from that recorded in the synoptic Gospels, still less to correct their dating of it. Rather, it would appear that he has set this well-known happening at the beginning of his Gospel and conjoined it with the sign of the changing of the water into wine in order to create a kind of program chapter: whoever understands the miracle of the Wine and the Cleansing of the Temple has the key to the ministry, death, and resurrection of Jesus and their outcome in the salvation of the kingdom and existence of the church.

In churches of our time the most common use of the story of Jesus at a wedding in Cana is to recount it on the occasion of a wedding, and so to convey from it a lesson for the happy couple. It tells of a bride and bridegroom whose marital troubles began even in the midst of their wedding celebrations; fortunately Jesus was at hand, and someone told him of the calamitous situation, and he put it right. The moral of the story is: When you find yourself in trouble, let Jesus know about it, and he will work things out for you; indeed, if you keep in touch with him he'll prevent you from getting into that sort of a mess! Such a use of the narrative, without simplistic conclusions, is naturally permissible, but we may be sure that that was far from the mind of the evangelist when he wrote it. The comment in John 2:11 indicates that the story has an intensely serious purpose: it is the first fulfillment of the declaration to the disciples in 1:51 (heaven is to pour out its blessings upon earth through the Son of Man) and so a revelation of the glory of Jesus.

The description in verses 2 and 3 of the presence of Jesus and his disciples at the wedding, and the failure of the wine to last is a hint of how such a catastrophe came about. A Jewish marriage feast, when the bride was a virgin, lasted for fully seven days. Such a custom was possible among poor people because the guests brought gifts, including provisions. Jesus and his disciples would have been viewed as a family for this purpose, but neither he nor they had gifts to bring; that will have occasioned Mary's drawing the attention of Jesus to the situation. It is hardly a plea for a miracle, but he had some responsibility for it, and surely he could do something to meet it!

His reply, "What have we to do with one another, woman?" uses familiar idiomatic speech and does not convey in a Jewish atmosphere the harshness that comes over in our language; it probably is intended to show that Jesus also shares his mother's concern. In the latter part of the Gospel the "hour" of Jesus denotes the time of his death (e.g., 7:30; 8:20, etc.), but here the statement that his hour had not yet come signifies rather his task of bringing the kingdom of God, which will culminate in his death and resurrection. That work has been given him by his Father, and the Father alone can determine when it begins, not his mother.

The mode of meeting the need of wine is clearly significant in a Jewish setting. Jars of water intended for ritual cleansing of people about to eat become, by the transforming power of Jesus, vessels of wine for celebrating the mercies of God. (Among pious Jews wine was almost exclusively used for religious purposes.) The meaning of the event is illuminated by one of the best known passages of the Bible of the Jews, and a favorite description of the kingdom of God in their eyes, namely Isaiah 25:6-9:

> The Lord of hosts will prepare a lavish banquet for all peoples on this mountain; a banquet of aged wine, choice pieces with marrow, and refined, aged wine. And on this mountain he will swallow up the covering

which is over all peoples, even the veil which is stretched over all nations. He will swallow up death for all time, and the Lord God will wipe tears away from all faces, and he will remove the reproach of his people from all the earth; for the Lord has spoken. And it will be said in that day, "Behold, this is our God for whom we have waited that he might save us. This is the Lord for whom we have waited; let us rejoice and be glad in his salvation" (NASB).

That celebration of the salvation of God's kingdom made its beginning in the peculiarly suitable setting of a wedding feast in Cana. Therein the glory of Jesus was manifested (v 11), and the "hour" of Jesus was adumbrated when the kingdom came for the deliverance of the whole human race—note that the feast of God is meant for "*all* peoples"! (Isa 25:6). The reality symbolized by the wine of the kingdom of God is none other than the "eternal life" of the kingdom, which was made known to Nicodemus (John 3:1–12), made possible by the lifting up of the Son of Man on his cross and to heaven (3:14, 15), and set forth for all humankind in the immortal words of John 3:16.

The Cleansing of the Temple does not strictly fall within our purview in this chapter, but its connection with the first sign warrants mention of it. In all four Gospels the event signifies less the action of a zealous reformer to purify the worship in the temple than an act of judgment (see Jer 7:4–15) that presaged a new and more worthy order of worship of God (cf. the anticipation of this in the kingdom of God, set forth in great detail in Ezek 40–48). That new order is achieved not by Jesus throwing the traders and their beasts out of the temple but by the death to which his action leads (note the citation of Psalm 69:9 in verse 17), and the resurrection which is inseparable from it.

This is made plain in the riddle-like utterance of John 2:19, spoken in reply to the demand of the Jewish leaders for a sign of his authority over the temple which, after all, was in their hands. "Destroy this temple" is an ironical call to the rulers to carry on as they have been doing, for that will surely lead to the destruction of their temple (note the close parallel in Matt 23:32–36). The sign that Jesus will then give will be to raise it "in three days." This prophecy perfectly accords with the Jewish expectation of a glorified temple in the kingdom of God. But in light of the impending death and resurrection of Jesus the "raising" of the temple "in three days" assumes a profounder meaning than the Jewish leaders could know. The "destruction" of the temple through the rejection of the Lord's Anointed (the "Messiah") primarily relates to its purpose as a place of meeting for God and the people. Since the rulers of the temple have rejected God in the person of his Son he rejects their temple (note Matt 23:38: "Behold, your house is being left to you—desolate!" And see the elaborate description of the abandonment of the temple by God in Ezek 10:15–19; 11:22, 23).

The new temple that Jesus is to raise is stated in verse 21 to be "the temple of his body." As the spiritual destruction of the old temple is brought about in the destruction of the body of Jesus so the building of the new temple is accomplished through the resurrection of Jesus. The risen Lord himself becomes the "place" where God is revealed, where his forgiveness and renewal are known, and where fellowship with God is experienced and forever maintained. Not *the church* as the "body" of Christ, but *the risen Lord in person* is the temple of the new order. That the symbolism can pass over to the church as the temple of the Lord, in view of the unity in the Spirit of the Lord and his people, is understandable (so in Rom 12:4, 5; 1 Cor 12:12, 13; and cf. 1 Pet 2:4, 5), but we must not impute it to this passage, where the Lord in his redemptive activity is explicitly in view. This is the root of the revelation expounded to the Samaritan woman—and to the church and the world at large—in John 4:21-24.

Two healings

In John 4:46-5:47 we have a typical example of the way the Book of Signs was constructed. Two stories are related of the miracle-working power of Jesus. One concerns a child who is desperately ill and about to die, the other a man advanced in years whose life has been ruined by illness. To both Jesus gives new life, and a discourse is added which draws out the implications of the signs.

What kind of a man was it who came to Jesus to request that he should heal his son? The term used to describe him, *basilikos*, is properly an adjective and means "what belongs to a king," and so "royal." As a noun it can be used to denote a member of a royal family, of the royal household, of the court, and of the king's army. Josephus uses the word in all these ways, and more than once he uses it in the plural, of the troops of the king's army. While therefore it is linguistically possible to translate the word here as a "royal official" (NIV, NASB) or "court official" (JB), it is most likely that this man was an officer in the army of Herod Agrippa. Perhaps he was the centurion of whom Matthew and Luke wrote, whose "boy" was ill and who showed great faith in Jesus (Matt 8:5-13; Luke 7:2-9). In that case the centurion will not have been a Roman, as is so commonly assumed, but in all probability an Arab.

Matthew speaks of the sick person as the soldier's *pais*. That is an ambiguous term; it can mean "boy" or "servant" (cf. the French *garçon*, boy, is still the usual term for "waiter" in a restaurant). Luke's source gave him the term *doulos*, "servant" or "slave." The original tradition doubtless spoke of the soldier's "boy," and the term was variously interpreted of his child or his servant. John makes it clear that he was his son, and that comports with the urgency of the officer in his approach to Jesus.

A further point of interest to note is that in both Matthew and John Jesus raises an objection to the father's request. Matt 8:17 is now commonly recognized to be a question: Jesus asks the officer, "Am I to come and heal him?" The officer had been long enough among Jews to know that Jews don't enter Gentile houses, since otherwise they would be rendered unclean. In John 4:48 Jesus responds to the officer's request with a heavy-hearted sigh: "Unless you people see signs and wonders you will never believe!" (Note the remarkable parallel to this in Mark 9:19, a similar situation of need.)

In Matthew the centurion expressed his great faith in asking Jesus simply to exercise his God-given authority and command the healing to take place; in John the officer was told to go home, since his son was alive, and he believed the word of Jesus and returned home without further question. The clue to the meaning of this incident is the statement, three times repeated, "your son lives" (see vv 50, 51, 53). Since it has been explicitly stated that the boy was at the point of death (v 47) the healing of the child is a sign of the power of Jesus to give life. In the discourse that follows this is spoken of as eternal life (5:24), and even resurrection life, which the Father has empowered the Son to bestow (5:21–29).

The Healing of the Paralytic at Bethesda (5:1–9) has essentially the same significance, even though the subject of healing is very different. The man in question has been ill for thirty-eight years, so presumably he was getting on in years. He was one of a number of pitiable physical wrecks lying by the pool of Bethesda, waiting for a miracle to happen to them (observe that the explanation of their presence at the pool is not in the earliest manuscripts of our Gospel, but it represents a popular

The Signs of Jesus and Their Significance

tradition noted by a later copyist in the margin of his manuscript). To judge from his response to the approach of Jesus, who sympathetically asked if he wanted to get well, the man had lost hope and faith as well as health. His reply was like that of many others in his condition—the complaint of an embittered spirit.

It is remarkable that Jesus selected such an individual as this among the many needy people waiting for a cure. The man had no idea who Jesus was; he didn't ask to be healed by him, and appears to have been altogether without faith. Nevertheless, Jesus took pity on him and with a word restored him to health. It is that very word spoken by Jesus to him that points to the significance of the healing: *Egeire*, i.e., "rise!" At the utterance of that word the paralytic was enabled to stand up, pick up his mattress, and walk. The healing was a sign of the truth of verse 21: "As the Father raises the dead (*egeirei*) and gives them life, so also the Son gives life to those whom he wishes." Jesus had given life to a man as good as dead. Such is the theme of the discourse in 5:16-30.

The discourse is sparked off by reference to the fact that the healing took place on the sabbath. Jewish leaders at the pool saw a man who had become a new creation by the power of God on the sabbath, but their gaze was entirely taken up with the mattress he was carrying. He was breaking the sabbath law! When the Jews learned that Jesus was the one who had both healed the man and commanded him to carry the mattress—both acts contrary to the sabbath law as they understood it—they were confirmed in their wrath against Jesus. Here was another example of Jesus acting as the law breaker! The tense of verse 16 should be observed: "It was on this account that the Jews used to persecute Jesus, because he used to do such things on the sabbath."

The response of Jesus to this criticism warrants closest attention: "My father has been working until now, and I also am working." This is a deliberate modification of the Jewish understanding of God's relation to the sabbath. Gen 2:2 states that God completed his work on the sixth day of creation, and so he rested on the seventh day. Since the works of creation were then finished, it was deduced that God's sabbath continues to this day. But that supposition raises a difficulty: How does one reconcile the thought that God keeps his sabbath with what the Scriptures say of his acts of judgment and salvation, e.g., in the Exodus? A popular answer to that question ran: God rested from work on the world, but not from his work on the godless and the righteous. He shows to the latter something of their recompense and to the former something of *their* recompense (so *Genesis Rabba* 11.8c).[2] In other words, God blesses the righteous in anticipation of their gaining the life of the kingdom of God and brings judgment on sinners in anticipation of their exclusion from it. Here then we see the significance of our Lord's words, ". . . and I'm working too." Jesus as Son of God does the works of God on the sabbath.

But the signs just described show that he brings to men no mere anticipation of the kingdom of God, but its reality—life from the dead! And he declares judgment on rejecters of the Word of God which the Last Judgment will confirm. That is spelled out in verses 24–29.

But there is a further element in the answer of Jesus in verse 17 that infuriated the Jewish leaders: "My *father* is working . . . and *I also am.*" Jesus, they said, was calling God his own Father, and thereby he was making himself equal with God. The former charge Jesus did not deny, but rather affirmed: Yes, God was his Father, and it was from him that his power and authority were derived. The second charge, however, Jesus rebutted. He did not make himself equal with God. He didn't make himself anything! Indeed, he could do *nothing* of himself! He depended utterly and entirely on his Father for his works. It was the Father who gave him power to give life to people, as the healing of the paralytic illustrated, and his

Father similarly has given him authority to judge humankind. Accordingly, to dishonor the Son is to dishonor the Father who sent him.

These insights with respect to the works of Jesus on the sabbath and his relation to the Father give insight into the heart of Jesus' understanding of his mission. His consciousness of unity with the Father combined with his sense of utter dependence on his Father is observable right through the Gospel. It characterizes the life of the incarnate Son of God, and his mission to bring life to all, from children (4:46–53) to the aged (5:1–9). But as Son of God he is the Mediator not only of life but of judgment. He makes it plain that the gospel he brings is a double-edged sword, and he demands that it be received responsibly.

The feeding of the multitude and walking on the sea

As in the preceding section, so here we have two signs followed by an explanatory discourse. Unlike the two former signs (but like the first recorded in the Gospel) these are "nature miracles," not healings of people. The discourse is almost wholly taken up with the meaning of the first sign. The second, however, is not ignored in the discourse, but rather contributes an essential element of its Christological basis.

The Feeding of the Multitude is the best known of the miracles of Jesus, and indeed it is the only miracle of his that is reported in all four Gospels. Not infrequently modern preachers tend to romanticize the event (when they don't render it innocuous!); attention is drawn more to the small boy who generously gave his lunch that others might share it than to the light that the event sheds on the Lord who multiplied the loaves. In reality it is a deeply theological narrative, closely linked with Old Testament story, type, and prophecy, with its center in Jesus, in whom earlier revelation and redemptive action comes to its completion.

The details of the event are familiar. Whereas the first three Gospels all mention that it took place in the wilderness, our evangelist merely mentions that it happened in the hill country on the other side of the lake from Galilee. Nevertheless he, as they, had the same fundamental conception in mind: The synoptists saw in the feeding miracle a repetition of the feeding of the people of God in the wilderness (see Exod 16:15-18, 31-36) but through a greater than Moses, the Christ of God; our evangelist assumes that understanding but emphasizes (through the discourse that follows) that Jesus, the Second Redeemer, was now bringing about the awaited second Exodus into the kingdom of God. The event, therefore, is recognized to be an anticipation of the feast of the kingdom of God for all nations (cf. Isa 25:6-9), but on a larger scale than the wedding in Cana of Galilee (2:1-11).

It is wholly characteristic of our evangelist, however, that by a mere mention of a date he orientates the event to the "hour" of Jesus, by which the nations will be able to participate in the feast of the kingdom. He notes, "The Passover, the great festival of the Jews, was near" (6:4). We shall consider at a later point the extent to which this reminder controls the interpretation of the sign; meanwhile we observe that Jesus' gift of the bread of the kingdom of God is related in the discourse to the bread that was "broken" in death and is broken every Lord's Day in the Lord's Supper.

It is inevitable that in discussions about the feeding miracle the question should rise as to what really happened on that occasion. The report in the Gospels of Jesus breaking five bread rolls and two pieces of dried fish on and on and on, till five thousand men were satisfied, is too frankly supernatural for many to accept. Various alternative explanations accordingly have been offered. It is suggested, e.g., that the sharing of one person's provisions was made by Jesus an example for others to follow, so that in the end nobody went hungry; or that the little that was available was broken into minute pieces, enabling a celebration of the eucharist to take place in the wilderness which was spiritually satisfying to all present; or even that an Old Testament story of a prophet feeding a group of hungry men (2 Kgs 4:42–44) was attributed to Jesus on an amplified scale. Such rationalizing explanations can be neither proved nor disproved, though all freely admit that they are out of harmony with the thought of the writers of the Gospels and of their sources.

In this connection one factor in John's description of the situation deserves to be weighed. He, and he alone of the evangelists, states that there was an almost revolutionary aftermath of the event. When the men present saw the "sign" that took place they concluded that Jesus must be the prophet that was to come into the world, i.e., the prophet like Moses, and they endeavored to seize Jesus and compel him to become king (verses 14, 15). In popular thought the "prophet like Moses" (Deut 18:15, 18) was to do the miracles that Moses did; some thought that Moses himself would return and lead Israel into a second exodus, but others identified the prophet with the expected Messiah.

Whatever the precise views of the multitude on this occasion, a full-blown messianic revolt centering on Jesus was about to take place. It was the most dangerous moment in the ministry of Jesus, threatening to undo all that he had sought to achieve through his preaching and demonstration of the real kingdom of God. His reaction is to be observed: some of our earliest manuscripts and witnesses to the Gospel text at this point read that Jesus "*fled* to the hills" (the reading, he "*departed* to the hills," is a later watering down of the text by copyists who could not believe that Jesus did such a thing). Plainly something more than a call by Jesus for generosity in sharing food or arranging for a kind of open-air eucharist was needed to account for that messianic "Revolt in the Desert" as Hugh Montefiore called it. We take it to be an act of God in Christ, as the other signs of Jesus were.

In Matthew and Mark, as well as in John, an account of Jesus' Walking on the Sea follows at once that of the feeding miracle. The fourth Gospel alone explains why Jesus sent his disciples away from the place: they, too, were Jews with messianic longings and aspirations and were as susceptible to messianic fervor as the rest (cf. Luke 19:11); it was essential that they should be removed from the dangerous situation that had arisen as speedily as possible. So Jesus went to the hills to pray and they were sent across the lake. As they rowed, the waters became increasingly whipped up by a powerful wind. Jesus therefore ceased his praying and went to their aid.

The text states that the disciples see Jesus "walking upon the sea and coming near the boat," and they were terrified. Did Jesus really do that? Some notable commentators, including Bernard, have pointed out that the language can mean that Jesus walked *beside* the sea, as in John 21:1. Bernard believed that John was correcting a false understanding of what actually took place: Jesus was walking beside the lake, and the disciples, not realizing that their boat had been driven close to the shore, thought that he was walking on the water, and in their fear they made a miracle out of a perfectly ordinary circumstance.

Linguistically, Bernard's view that *"epi tes thalasses"* can mean "beside the sea" is correct, but his interpretation of what John was wanting to say is quite certainly far from the evangelist's mind. Mark uses exactly the same wording as John, and he goes on to say that the boat was *"in the midst of* the sea" (Mark 6:47). Matthew is equally clear and emphatic in his account (Matt 14:25).

In John 21:1ff. the situation described is wholly different; there the evangelist plainly states that Jesus stood "on the beach," and he goes on to tell of the conversation of Jesus with the disciples in that place. If John had wished to correct the churches' (mis)understanding of what Jesus was doing on or beside the sea he could have easily done so by writing unambiguously that Jesus was walking *alongside* the sea (*para ten thalassan*). Precisely this phrase occurs in Mark 1:14 and Acts 10:6. In reality it is this extraordinary situation that gives rise to the utterance of Jesus which forms the reason for the evangelist telling the story: "Stop being afraid," said Jesus: "*I am (he).*" The expression "I am" is reproduced elsewhere by John (see especially John 8:24, 28, 58; 13:19), and he intends us to recall the name of the Lord revealed to Moses in the wilderness (Exod 3:14) as well as in the prophetic writings (see especially the central chapters of Isaiah, notably Isa 43:10, 25). The evangelist, when describing the present event, will doubtless have had in mind the description of God coming to the rescue of the Israelite tribes at the Red Sea in Psalm 77:16, 19 (NIV):

> The waters saw you, O God,
> the waters saw you and writhed;
> the very depths were convulsed . . . .
> Your path led through the sea,
> your way through the mighty waters,
> though your footprints were not seen.

So the evangelist saw Jesus, the revelation of the Father, coming to his disciples in their distress—in the Second Exodus!

The discourse that now follows is almost wholly taken up with the meaning of the sign of the Feeding of the Multitude, but the Walking on the Sea is also presupposed. It is because Jesus can utter, "I am" that he can also say, "I am the Bread of Life" (6:35). An odd feature of the discourse is that it begins beside the lake (v 25) and ends in the synagogue at Capernaum (v 59). At some point in it a change of venue is presupposed. This could throw light on an element in the discourse to which we earlier alluded. In verses 25-29 Jesus addresses the men who had followed him after the miracle in the wilderness, telling them to seek the bread that endures to eternal life which he, the Son of Man, gives. In verses 30ff. certain Jews ask what work Jesus does that can compare with the gift of bread from heaven that Moses gave and that the Messiah shall give, and they challenge him to do the same. It is evident that they had heard reports of the feeding of the crowd, and they disbelieved them and so opposed him, probably in the synagogue of Capernaum.

The chief features of the discourse that especially relate to the sign of the feeding miracle are: (i) the affirmation of Jesus that he is the Bread of Life that satisfies the hunger of humankind (v 35); (ii) he, unlike the manna that God gave, is the *real* Bread that came down from heaven and gives life to the world, an assertion that implies his incarnation as the Son of God (vv 32, 33); (iii) the Bread that Jesus gives is his flesh for the life of the world, hence he must die to impart the living bread to the human family (v 51); (iv) the violent symbol of the necessity of eating his flesh and drinking his blood is employed (vv 53-58), emphasizing that it is needful not only to *come* to Jesus, and to *believe* on him, but to *receive* him—all which are really different aspects of faith. For Jesus is both the giver of the living Bread and is the living Bread. This revelation is perfectly comprehensible to the people of the new covenant as they celebrate its truth in the Lord's Supper. In its essentials it can be grasped by any who reach the faith of Peter that Jesus is the Holy One of God and has the words of eternal life (vv 68, 69).

The healing of the man born blind

This graphic story is one of the most fascinating in the four Gospels. The account of the healing is briefly given in verses 1–7, and the rest of the chapter tells of its consequences. Throughout the narrative the blind man is on center stage, and the evangelist tells the story by recounting the differing reactions of people to his changing situations. He begins with the reactions of the disciples of Jesus to the man's blindness (vv 1, 2) and the contrasting response of Jesus to it (vv 3–5). He continues with the astonishment of the man's neighbors (vv 8–12), the hostility of the Jewish leaders (vv 13–24), and the bewilderment and fear of the man's parents (vv 19–23). The compassion of Jesus on the now outcast man concludes the healing narrative (vv 35–38), but a postscript is added: Jesus' mission is to make blind to see and seeing blind (vv 39–41).

The disciples' response to the sight of the blind man is typical of the world of their day, including the Jews. It was generally believed that all suffering was due to sin, hence all sufferers were punished for their sins. The Jerusalem Targum on Deut 21:20 states that parents bringing a rebellious son to the elders should say, "We have transgressed the Word of the Lord, *therefore* this our son has been born to us, who is unruly and rebellious." The possibility of a child sinning before birth was also discussed by the rabbis. They were intrigued by the mention in Gen 25:22 of the twins Jacob and Esau struggling in Rebekah's womb. One rabbi suggested that they went round trying to kill one another. Someone else had the bright idea that when Rebekah walked past a synagogue Jacob struggled to get out (on the basis of Jer 1:5), but when Rebekah passed an idol temple Esau struggled to get out (cf. Psalm 58:4)! Jesus dismissed such speculations. This man's plight, he said, was not due to his or his parents' sin; it was that the man might have a share in the mission of the Son of God and that the glory of his salvation be revealed in him. He was to become a demonstration of the truth that Jesus is the Light of the world (v 5).

The mode of Jesus' Healing of the Blind Man reminds us of Mark 8:23; doubtless his actions helped encourage the faith of the man. The latter was sent to wash in the pool of Siloam, as Elisha sent Naaman to wash in the Jordan to heal his leprosy (2 Kgs 5:10–14). But saliva, mud, and washing in a pool make no blind person to see; it is the word and power of Jesus that do that. The evangelist sees this illustrated in the meaning of the name *Siloam*. It puts in a Greek form the Hebrew *Shiloaḥ*, which is a participle meaning "sent." The term related to the waters that were "sent" (i.e., gushed) into the pool, but in the Gospel the evangelist repeatedly mentions that Jesus is the "Sent One" of God. The blind man receives his sight as he washes in the pool named "Sent," but he is healed by the Sent One of God. Jesus is, as John Chrysostom put it, the "spiritual Siloam."

The neighbors of the blind man could not believe the evidence of their eyes as they looked on the beggar they knew, but who now saw. They took him to the Pharisees, who were their spiritual leaders and who ought to know about this miracle. The Pharisees, however, were nonplused. The healing had taken place on the sabbath; the miracle pointed to Jesus as an instrument of God, but its occurrence on the sabbath showed him to be a sinner! They therefore sent for the man's parents, to see if the healing were genuine. The parents were ready enough to attest the blindness of their son and the fact of his healing, but they were unwilling to say more for fear of being thrown out of the synagogue.

The accuracy of that observation has been questioned by some scholars. We know that about the end of the first century of our era the daily prayers of the Jews (used also in all synagogue services) included a curse on the Christians. It ran:

Let the Nazarenes and the heretics be destroyed in a moment, and let them be blotted out of the book of life and not be inscribed with the righteous.

The Signs of Jesus and Their Significance

It is believed that this prayer was intended to bring about the exclusion of all Jewish Christians from the synagogue, something that did not take place in the time of Jesus and the early church. The evangelist, it is suggested, was reflecting in this story what went on in his day, and was really addressing his contemporaries through it. Undoubtedly John was relating this event to the Christians of his day, but he was doing the same in every line of his Gospel. In reality he had justification for his statement in this case. Jesus himself warned against being afraid to confess faith in him before men (Mark 8:37), and he pronounced a blessing on those who endured persecution, were hated, insulted, excluded, and rejected because of their connection with him (Luke 6:22; Matt 5:11, 12). The book of Acts illustrates the situation of the blind man and his parents, and of Christians generally. The curse on the Nazarenes was but a reinforcement of the attitude of Jewish authorities toward followers of Jesus from the time of the ministry of Jesus onward.

The rest of the narrative shows the Pharisees endeavoring to discredit the testimony of the blind man. They command him to "give glory to God," i.e., by confessing the truth (cf. Jos 7:19). Thus, they were implying that he was a liar, that Jesus was a sinner, and that they were right. He confessed the truth readily enough—that once he was blind, but now he can see! And he confessed his amazement at the rulers' ignorance of Jesus and their disbelief in the good he was doing. Outraged at this the Pharisees exclaimed, "You were born in utter sin, and are you trying to instruct us?" So then they admitted that he was born blind! And that Jesus must have healed him! But they rejected him, and the miracle, and the one who performed it.

When Jesus heard what had happened to the man he found him, and completed the process of his healing, opening his spiritual eyes to know who it was who had healed him. This was the first time the blind man saw Jesus, and he now learned that he was looking into the face of the Son of Man. No wonder he fell down before him and gave him glory!

The conclusion of the story is an ironical but somber utterance of Jesus: "for judgment I came into this world . . . ." We cannot but contrast John 3:17. Salvation is the primary intent of the coming of Jesus, but since salvation calls for faith and obedience, rejection of the saving revelation entails God's rejection of the rejecter. The Light of the world shows up the darkness, and the way out of it. They who refuse to see the Light are confirmed in their blindness (9:40, 41).

The raising of Lazarus

A feature of the Lazarus account strikes the observant reader immediately. Instead of its describing a sign of Jesus followed by an exposition of its meaning, it reads like a narrative interspersed with comments that reveal its meaning step by step. There is truth in that observation, although the major elements in the story actually occur at the beginning and the end, and the intermediate steps are punctuated by conversations of Jesus, notably with the disciples (vv 7–16), with Martha (vv 20–27), and with Mary (vv 28–32).

The raising to life of a dead person by Jesus is not a solitary occurrence in the Gospels. His message to John the Baptist, who had inquired whether he was indeed the Messiah, includes in a brief summary of his works, "the dead are raised" (Matt 11:5). Note the plural! The synoptic Gospels tell of the raising of Jairus's daughter (Mark 5:21–24, 35–43) and of the widow's son in Nain (Luke 7:11–17). In the case of Lazarus, however, Jesus is confronted with a situation in which a man had been dead for four days—manifestly beyond all possibility of recall by a kiss of life. In the raising of Lazarus we meet with the starkest expression of God at work through Jesus among people in the extremity of need.

The statement of Jesus on learning of Lazarus's illness provides a clue as to how we are to understand what now takes place: "This illness is . . . for the sake of the glory of God, that the Son of God may be glorified through it" (v 4). In this Gospel the glorifying of God through the Son primarily takes place in the event when the Son is glorified by God, namely as he is lifted up via his cross to heaven. Jesus, on his way to his death, awakens a dead man. His life-giving work becomes the occasion of his giving up his own life, as the postscript to the story shows (11:47–53).

The extraordinary observation in verses 5 and 6 is probably to be linked with this understanding of the event. Jesus, comments John, loved Martha and Mary and Lazarus; when therefore he heard that Lazarus was ill he remained where he was two days more! The conundrum is illuminated by verses 11 and 17: The messenger from the sisters will have taken a day to reach Jesus; Jesus waits two more days; he takes another day to reach Bethany, and is told that Lazarus had died four days earlier. Jesus will have realized on the messenger's arrival that Lazarus was already beyond healing and was dead. His delay accordingly was for the even greater glory of God, the greater blessing of the family of Lazarus (though they could not yet know it), and the greater revelation of the saving power of God through his Son.

The conversation of Jesus with Martha is the most important in the chapter. Her opening words are not a rebuke but a simple expression of grief and continuing faith in Jesus. His affirmation that her brother will rise is accepted as a consolatory reminder of the hope of resurrection in the last day. But Jesus has more than the last day in view: He illumines that day with the light of the present kingdom of God and the presence of the king: "I am the resurrection . . . " The power to raise the dead has been vested in him, hence the believer in him "even though he dies will come to life." The believer's resurrection is assured by the Lord of the resurrection.

But more: "Everyone who *lives and believes in me* will never, never die!" The believer in Jesus "lives" even now, i.e., he has the life of the kingdom of God, and over that life death has no power. Of the truth and the nature of this specifically Christian hope the resurrection of Lazarus is the sign. The conversation with Mary is much briefer, but it leads to a statement of the evangelist as surprising as anything in his Gospel. "When Jesus saw her weeping, and the Jews who had come with her weeping, he became angry in spirit and very agitated" (v 33). Virtually every English translation of the Bible waters that down to mean that Jesus was "deeply moved" in spirit, but the lexicographers and the great commentators protest that that is not what John meant.

Rudolf Schnackenburg, the greatest contemporary scholar on John's Gospel, wrote:

> The word . . . indicates an outburst of anger, and any attempt to reinterpret it in terms of an internal emotional upset caused by grief, pain, or sympathy is illegitimate.[3]

The anger of Jesus was due not to Lazarus's death but the behavior of his relatives and friends over his death. To use Paul's language, they sorrowed "like the rest of men who have no hope" (1 Thess 4:13). Despite the Old Testament, despite the signs of Jesus attesting the kingdom of God among them, and despite his own teaching they mourned like the pagans. It was this unbelief of the people of God in the presence of him who is the Resurrection and the Life, and who had come to raise Lazarus from death, that made Jesus angry. The same comment is repeated by the evangelist as Jesus approached the grave of Lazarus (v 38). Why, then, did Jesus weep (v 35)? His tears, if not caused by the unbelief that made him angry, will have been evoked by the sight of the havoc created by sin and death, the tragedy of the human situation in which even the people of God are engulfed.

And so Jesus comes to the tomb. He commands the stone to be removed from it, despite Martha's expression of horror. Then he prays. But there is no petition, simply a brief giving of thanks that his Father had "heard" him, i.e., had listened to him and granted his request. The praying had already been done! There was no need to pray more. Accordingly Jesus calls Lazarus with a great shout—"Lazarus, come out here!" It was like the shout of the archangel and the trumpet of God (1 Thess 4:16), and it had a similar effect. Lazarus came out, shuffling in his grave clothes. At the word of Jesus the bystanders released him from them, and Lazarus was free to live again.

That the evangelist's selection of the signs of Jesus should end with the account of the raising of Lazarus is entirely fitting, not only because of its stupendous nature, or because it was chronologically the last, but above all by reason of its meaning. More plainly than any other sign of Jesus it brings into relief the meaning of them all, namely that Jesus is the Redeemer, who by his living, working, dying, and rising brings to all humankind the life of the kingdom of God. Moreover it makes transparently clear that in order for this life of the kingdom to come to the world Jesus must give his own life—and take it again! (see John 10:17, 18).

It is John who informs us that the raising of Lazarus was the last straw for the Jewish Sanhedrin. It led them to approve the high priest's recommendation that Jesus must die that the whole nation should not perish (11:49, 50). The later trial of Jesus was but the formal ratification of that decision. But as the evangelist noted, the high priest's words are an extraordinary unconscious prophecy. Its language is strangely reminiscent of the gospel summary in John 3:16. The signs of Jesus illumine the multifaceted truth of that summary and encourage all to experience it for themselves.

4   JESUS AND THE JEWISH FESTIVALS

The religious life of the Jews was regulated by a complex institution of festivals or obligatory religious occasions. The term "feast" conveys a misleading notion to modern ears. The fundamental festival was the sabbath day, hardly a day characterized by feasting. That day was ordained as "a sabbath to the Lord" (Exod 20:8-11), a rest day in his honor. Every new moon was counted as a festival (Num 10:10), the seventh new moon being observed with particular solemnity (Lev 23:24, 25), doubtless because of its number. So also the seventh year was viewed as "a sabbath of rest for the land" (Exod 23:11). The passage of seven sevens of years led to the celebration of the so-called Year of Jubilee (Lev 25:8-55), which came to be viewed as a type or foreshadowing of the kingdom of God (Isa 61:1, 2; cf. Luke 4:16-21).

In addition, there were festal celebrations of a special kind, often called "pilgrim feasts" (the Hebrew term for feast, ḥag, was related to the verb ḥagag, meaning "to make a pilgrimage"). The Old Testament specifies three of these, which were to be attended by all the men of Israel:

Three times a year all your men must appear before the Lord your God at the place he will choose: at the Feast of Unleavened Bread, the Feast of Weeks and the Feast of Tabernacles.
(Deut 16:16 NIV; note the slightly different wording of Exod 23:14)

Originally these were all agricultural festivals, but to each of them a special significance was attached, for in them the people celebrated particular aspects of God's dealing with his people in the sacred history. The festival of Unleavened Bread was preceded by the Passover, commemorating Israel's deliverance from Egypt. The festival of the Harvest ("Weeks") memorialized the giving of the Law, and the Ingathering ("Tabernacles") was especially associated with the wilderness wanderings of the people.

Two other festivals came to be observed in the period shortly before the first century of our era—the festival of the Dedication and Purim. The former was instituted by Judas Maccabaeus to commemorate the cleansing of the temple after its desecration by Antiochus Epiphanes, and is the context of a dialogue between Jews and Jesus in John 10. The latter was a lively celebration of the deliverance of Israel from Haman through Esther and Mordecai, but is not mentioned in the New Testament.

One of the outstanding differences between the synoptic Gospels and John is that the former record one visit only of Jesus to celebrate a pilgrim festival in Jerusalem, and that in the last week of his life, whereas John tells of Jesus attending all the major feasts (other than Purim). Moreover, while the synoptists doubtless assumed the profound significance of the Passover festival in relation to the death of Jesus, they nowhere elaborate it, whereas the fourth evangelist makes a point of linking these feasts to the redemption brought by Jesus. The festivals of Israel to a marked degree enshrined the heritage, faith, and hope of Israel; John is anxious to demonstrate that by his word and action Jesus represents the fulfillment of the festivals, and consequently the fulfillment of the heritage, faith, and hope of Israel. To the consideration of the outworking of this theme we now turn.

The Passover Festival

The Passover was the first of Israel's festivals in the liturgical year, and, as it happens, the first to be mentioned in the fourth Gospel (2:13). It is possible that, like the other Jewish feasts, the Passover had an earlier history, maybe a shepherd's rite when the Israelite tribes were nomadic shepherds. But it was given a unique significance through relating it to Israel's deliverance from Egypt, just as the Passover itself became transformed into the Christian Lord's Supper.

In New Testament times the Passover lambs were bought and then handed to the priests to be slaughtered by them in the temple. This took place in the early afternoon; then the lambs were handed back to the persons to whom they belonged for the Passover celebration in the evening. The lamb was eaten with bitter herbs dipped in a paste of fruit and nuts.

At an appropriate point in the meal the appointed "son" (the group might not be a real family) asked the question, "Why is this night different from all other nights?" The answer was given in accordance with Exod 12:26 and 27, and Exod 13:3–16: The Lord's deliverance of the Israelites from the Egyptians was recounted, followed by remembrance of later experiences of the Lord's salvation, and prayer was made for a comparable deliverance from the oppressive power of Rome. The place of hope for Israel's future salvation in the celebration of the Passover has already been noted. The expectation of a second Exodus under the second Redeemer, the Messiah, was a living hope in Israel during the time of

Jesus and the early church. It features prominently in the fourth Gospel and in the book of Revelation.

When considering the sign of the feeding of the multitude we observed the note of time in John 6:4: "The Passover, . . . of the Jews, was near," and we reflected on the likelihood that this was intended as a key to the meaning of the sign. E. C. Hoskyns expressed this in a typical compressed sentence:

> The movement from the miracle to the discourse, from Moses to Jesus, and above all from bread to flesh, is almost unintelligible unless the reference in verse 4 to the passover picks up 1:29, 36, anticipates 19:36 (Exod 12:46; Num 9:12) and governs the whole narrative.[1]

The discourse, as far as verse 35, is comprehensible in terms of the gift of manna given by the Messiah in the second Exodus. Jews frequently used the symbolism of eating and drinking with regard to receiving the instruction of the Law and Wisdom (to the rabbis the two were the same). Ben Sira writes in the name of Wisdom (Ecclus 24:21):

> Whoever feeds on me will be hungry for more,
> Whoever drinks from me will thirst for more.

He then proceeds to identify Wisdom and the Law. John 6:38-50 develops the thought that the "bread" is he who came down from heaven to reveal the Father. The manna came from heaven; the Son of God came from heaven. From verse 51 on, however, the "bread" is nothing other than the flesh of Jesus, given for the life of the world. "Flesh," "given," "on behalf of"—this is sacrificial language. Jesus the Bread of God is to die as the Lamb of God for the sin of the world (John 1:29). He is God's Passover Lamb.

The symbolism of eating the flesh of the Son of Man is a natural extension of the concept of Jesus as God's Passover Lamb, but the thought of drinking the blood of the Son of Man is a development of the fundamental imagery of verse 35 in the light of verse 51: "coming" and "believing" are replaced by "eating" and "drinking." In both cases the object of faith is Christ in his sacrificial offering of his body and blood for the life of the world.

The language, admittedly, at first hearing will have been shocking to the Jew, but in the context of the Last Supper of Jesus and the Lord's Supper of the church it is entirely comprehensible. Adolf Schlatter's comment on this passage is worth reflecting on:

> What we have to do with his flesh and blood is not chew and swallow, but recognize in his crucified body and poured out blood the ground of our life, and hang our faith and hope on that body and blood and draw from there our thinking and our willing.[2]

The symbolic imagery of eating and drinking is more widely used than we sometimes think. We can speak of devouring a book, drinking in the substance of an address, swallowing a story (or declining to do so!), chewing over a matter, ruminating over an idea (to ruminate is to chew the cud!). Sometimes we say that we cannot stomach an idea, or even a particular person. And I have heard a fond grandmother declare that she could eat her grandbaby! Such language, strange as it may seem, is not uncommon in Eastern religions with regard to sharing in the being of God. The most pertinent example of this imagery occurs in the Talmud. A certain Rabbi Hillel (not the famous rabbi of that name) shocked his contemporaries by saying: "There shall be no Messiah for Israel, because they have already eaten him in the days of Hezekiah."[3]

Hillel may have wished to counter the apocalyptic ideas of some of his contemporaries, or more likely to oppose the preaching of the Christians. In any case he appears to have thought that Hezekiah fulfilled the role of the Messiah in light of the ministry of Isaiah and the marvelous deliverance of Israel from the power of the Assyrians. It is noteworthy that the English translation of the Talmud substitutes the term "enjoyed" for "eaten." The blessings awaited from the Messiah were enjoyed by Israel through king Hezekiah's rule. When Jesus and the church use this language, however, it is more intensely personal. The meaning is well expressed in John 6:57: "Just as the living Father sent me and I live because of the Father, so whoever eats me will live because of me." The believer depends on and is sustained by the Son as the Son in his life depended upon and was sustained by the Father.

In the account of the trial and crucifixion of Jesus several passages have the evident intention of relating the death of Jesus to the Passover. When the Jewish leaders hand Jesus over to the Roman governor for trial it is recorded: "they did not enter the Governor's residence so as not to become defiled, but that they might eat the passover lamb" (18:28). The irony of the situation is evident: The Jewish leaders hold firmly to the ceremonial law while they are bent on bringing about the execution of Israel's promised Deliverer, the Messiah-Son of God. In their zeal to eat the Passover they unknowingly help to fulfill its ultimate meaning in the sacrifice of the Lamb of God.

A comparable note of the time in Jesus' trial is given in John 19:14. When Pilate recognized that his efforts to release Jesus were of no avail he took his place on the judge's seat. The evangelist observes, "It was the Preparation Day for the Passover, the hour was about midday. . . ." The evangelist is conscious that this is a momentous hour in world history. But it was significant also for the Jews, for at this hour they ceased their work, the leaven was gathered out of the houses, and the Passover lambs were being prepared for slaughter. The festival was virtually beginning and its fulfillment in the setting apart of the Lamb of God for his sacrifice was under way.

This relating of the death of Jesus to the Passover comes to its climax in an eyewitness account of the crucifixion, described in John 19:31–37. The Jewish leaders had requested Pilate to have the three crucified men killed and buried, so that their bodies should not remain exposed during the Passover festival and so defile the land. The request was granted. Soldiers advanced to the crucified men and "broke" the legs of two of them. The action was more brutal than the description; the custom was to smash the legs of the crucified with an iron mallet, so causing great loss of blood and asphyxia. The men died at once. The soldiers went to Jesus with the intention of doing the same, but on approaching him they saw that he was already dead, and so had no need of this treatment. One soldier accordingly thrust his lance into the side of Jesus, presumably to make sure he really was dead; an efflux of blood and water immediately took place.

At this point in his record the evangelist adds an emphatic declaration of the truth of his account: It rests on the evidence of an eyewitness whose trustworthiness all acknowledge. And he makes a comment: "These events happened in order that the scripture might be fulfilled, 'Not a bone of his is to be broken.' And again another scripture says, 'They will look on him whom they pierced.'" The latter citation is from Zechariah 12:10, describing the grief and repentance of the Jewish people for their treatment of God's representative, and the subsequent opening of a fountain for cleansing their sin (in Matt 24:30 and Rev 1:7 the Scripture is applied to the nations generally).

The evangelist includes this reference probably to demonstrate the reality of the death of Jesus, and so the reality of his humanity in face of those who in his day wished to deny it (cf. 1 John 4:1-6, 5:6-9). The former citation is found, with more or less approximation to the wording, in no less than three Old Testament passages. In Exod 12:46 and Num 9:12 it refers to the way in which the Passover lamb should be eaten: "not a bone of it shall be broken," i.e., in the roasting and eating of it. In Ps 34:20 the words relate to God's care for the Righteous Sufferer: "He protects all his bones, not one of them will be broken" (NIV). The evangelist will quite certainly have known both these applications of the words he cites. In light of the importance to him of the Passover typology the application to the Passover lamb will have been foremost in his mind: Jesus in his death brings to fulfillment the significance of the Passover in relation to the present and the future; through his sacrificial death and risen life he enacts the Second Exodus and opens for all mankind the promised kingdom of God. At the same time he fulfills the role of the Righteous Man, who suffers on behalf of the unrighteous but remains at all times in the care of God—a care that results in resurrection to his presence and Lordship over the kingdom.

The Festival of Weeks

The second pilgrim festival of the Jewish year was variously named by the Jews. In Exod 23:16 it is called "the Festival of the Harvest." In Deut 16:10 it has the name "Festival of Weeks," doubtless due to the command to count seven weeks from the day after Passover and to celebrate the festival on the fiftieth day. This command, however, led Jews outside Palestine to give it the name "Pentecost," a Greek term which simply means "fiftieth." The festival lasted one day, although in the world outside Palestine it generally lasted two days (to be sure that it was celebrated on the right day!). The agricultural aspect of the festival in later times gave place to observance of the day in celebration of the giving of the Law. R. Eleazar ben Pedath in the third century A.D. stated, "Pentecost is the day on which the Torah was given." To this day it is known among Jews as "the time of the giving of our Law." There is evidence that it was so observed in the time of Jesus and the early church.

The festival is not mentioned by name in the fourth Gospel. But from very early times it was realized that the unnamed festival in John 5:1 was the Festival of Weeks, i.e., Pentecost. The identification fits perfectly the content of the discourse in the chapter. The emphasis throughout the discourse is on the authority of Jesus. As Son of God he does what the Father does, for the Father shows him and teaches him to do his works, which include raising the dead and the exercise of judgment (5:21-29).

The latter half of the discourse is a self-contained unit. It reminds us of the trial scenes in the Old Testament, when the Lord calls witnesses from the nations to testify on behalf of their gods in face of the overwhelming truth of the only God, whose witnesses the people of Israel are (see, e.g., Isa 43:8-13; 44:6-11). Here Jesus is opposed by Jews, who ask for witnesses to justify his claims. He proceeds to call them, beginning with "Another," an unnamed person but whose witness John knows to be true (5:32). That "Other" is God himself, who has provided witness through John the Baptist (vv 33-35), the works of Jesus (v 36), and the Word of God in the Scriptures (vv 37-40). It is important to note that in verse 37 the witness of the Father to Jesus is not through his voice but through the Scriptures, which the opponents of Jesus do not grasp. They "search the Scriptures," believing that in so doing they possess the life of which they speak. But they are wrong! To read and study the Scriptures is not the equivalent of swallowing spiritual vitamins that give eternal life; they are given as the Father's witness to Jesus, that people who read them may repent and believe on him, and so receive from him the eternal life promised in the Scriptures.

The upshot of this is an astonishing turn of the tables. The Jews believed that Moses, who interceded for their fore-fathers when they worshiped the golden calf (Exod 32:30–32), continues to be their intercessor in heaven (so in the *Assumption of Moses*, 12:6). On this basis they looked for him to intercede for them at the last judgment, and so they set their hope on him (see John 5:45). Jesus declared that, on the contrary, Moses was their accuser, not defender, for "he wrote about me," and "if you are not believing his writings, how will you believe my words?" Since the Law, in Jewish eyes, is the supreme element in the Scriptures, Moses must be accounted as the supreme witness to Jesus; accordingly on the day that the Jews celebrated the giving of the Law they should the more readily receive his witness and the Word of God that Jesus brings.

The Pentecostal festival thus gains its ultimate significance in the witness of the Law, Prophets, and Writings to Jesus and his mission from God. To celebrate the festival in the right way is to listen to their testimony and seek from Jesus the life of the kingdom of God of which the Scriptures speak.

The Festival of Tabernacles

This festival, which began on the fifteenth day of the seventh month (September/October), was primarily a thanksgiving for the harvests of wine, fruit, and olives. This feature was combined with thankful remembrance of the blessings of God upon his people during the forty years of wanderings in the wilderness together with an anticipation of their renewal at the second Exodus, when the kingdom of God should come. "Tabernacle" is an old English word (derived from the Latin *tabernaculum*) meaning a hut or shed or booth. "Festival of Tabernacles," thus, is simply the "festival of tents." All who kept it camped out in shelters of leafy branches set on housetops or around houses or in fields, so vividly recalling the time when their forefathers lived for a whole generation under the open sky.

John 7 and 8 are set in this festival, and the central utterances of Jesus are clearly related to the outstanding events of the festival. The structure of signs-plus-discourse elsewhere in the Gospel is replaced by festival rites-plus-teaching of Jesus concerning them.

Each day at dawn priests, accompanied by the festival crowds, went in procession from the temple to the pool of Siloam. There an appointed priest filled a golden pitcher with water and carried it back to the temple. The psalm of the kingdom in Isa 12 was sung, with its central words, "With joy you will draw water from the wells of salvation."

The priests processed round the altar, and the temple choir sang the *Hallel* (Psalms 113–118), supported at appropriate times with the shouts of the men and boys, "Give thanks to the Lord!" and "O Lord, save us!" and the shaking of branches. The priest who had drawn the water mounted the altar and poured the daily drink offering of wine into a bowl and then the water from Siloam into another. The crowd shouted, "Lift up your hand!" as a sign that the offering was completed.

The whole procedure had in mind the gift of water in the desert when the Jews were in danger of dying of thirst (Exod 17:1-6), and the prophecy of a river of living water flowing from the Jerusalem temple in the kingdom of God (Ezek 47:1-11) plus that of waters in the new age flowing from Jerusalem to the eastern and western seas (Zech 14:8). These passages of Scripture were all read in the festival.

The burning question that none can answer is at what time Jesus uttered John 7:37, 38. The saying is best rendered as follows:

Jesus and the Jewish Festivals

"If anyone is thirsty, let him come to me,
and let him drink who believes in me.
As the scripture said,
'Rivers of living water will flow from his heart.'"

If the voice of Jesus sounded across the temple court immediately after the crowd had shouted, "Lift up your hand!" and the priest had done so, the cry of Jesus would have been as a thunder clap from heaven. Even had it been at a later hour, or on the eighth day when no ritual drawing of water took place, the significance of the cry would have been plain to all. Jesus was claiming to fulfill the meaning and promise of the festival for his people. As God rescued the fathers in the desert by giving them water, so Jesus can do for his generation. And as the Jews looked to God to send the river of living water from his presence in the kingdom of God, so Jesus offers the living water in the present, for he is the Mediator of the life of the kingdom. (Note, the water flows from Jesus the Representative of God and Savior, not from the believer; in Ezek 47 it comes from God, and in Rev 22:1 and 2 it flows from the throne of God and the Lamb.)

The evangelist is conscious that the present gift offered as Jesus was speaking required for its fullness the "lifting up" of Jesus (on his cross to the throne of God) and the outpouring of the Holy Spirit of the kingdom (John 7:39); but this the reader of the Gospel on this side of Easter and Pentecost fully understood. And we modern readers can understand how astonished the temple police sent to arrest Jesus were on hearing these words; they could no more lay hands on Jesus than they could have attempted to lay hands on God Almighty! But more was to follow.

The next sentence from Jesus recorded by the evangelist is in John 8:12. It has been separated from the narrative of chapter 7 by the story of the woman caught in the act of adultery. This account is not in the earliest manuscripts of our Gospel but occurs in various places in the Gospels and has evidently come from an independent source. Accordingly, 8:12 belongs (with 7:37, 38) to the festival of the Tents. The background to this utterance is given in the Talmudic tractate:

> Toward the end of the feast of Tabernacles, people went down into the court of the women. . . . Golden lamps were there, and four golden bowls were on each of them, and four ladders were by each; four young men from the priestly group of youths had jugs of oil in their hands and poured oil from them into the individual bowls. Wicks were made from the discarded trousers of the priests and from their girdles. There was no court in Jerusalem that was not bright from the light of the place of drawing water. Men of piety and known for their good works danced before them with torches in their hands, and sang before them songs and praises. And the Levites stood with zithers and harps and cymbals and trumpets and other musical instruments without number. . . .

This procedure happened every night of the festival, except on an intervening sabbath. It was intended to recall the pillar of cloud by day and of fire by night that was with the Israelites in the wilderness, a sign of the presence of God. It had saved them from threatened destruction by the Egyptian army (Exod 14:19–25) and led them through the wilderness to the promised land. The lighted lamps also brought to mind the promise of the shining of the light of God for their salvation in the coming kingdom of God (cf. Isa 60:14–22; Zech 14:5–7).

In affirming "I am the Light of the world" Jesus was again appropriating the symbolism of the festival to show the fulfillment of the history and hope of God's people in his

God-appointed ministry. As Israel followed the Light from the land of slavery through the wilderness to the promised land, so the believer following Jesus has "the Light of life." He has both the promise of life in the kingdom to come and its possession now. Jesus fulfills Tabernacles!

The Festival of the Dedication

There is no reference in the Old Testament to the Dedication Festival. It had its origin at a later time, in one of the most astonishing and courageous episodes of the history of Israel. Antiochus Epiphanes, one of the successors of Alexander the Great, endeavored to unify his empire by establishing a single religion throughout its borders. In accordance with this policy he ordered the Jews to give up their religion and its laws and to adopt the worship of Zeus.

The climax of his religious reformation was to set on the great altar in the temple of Jerusalem a pagan altar, on which stood an image of Zeus bearing his likeness. And on the twenty-fifth of Kislev (i.e., December) 167 B.C. a sacrifice of pigs was offered on this altar. The turmoil and suffering that this attempted forced apostasy caused in Israel can well be imagined. In an incredible series of battles with the forces of Antiochus, Judas the Maccabee ("the Hammerer"!) led the Jews to victory. And on the twenty-fifth of Kislev 164 B.C., three years to the day, the desecrated temple was cleansed and sacrifice was offered in accordance with the Law.

The people rapturously celebrated the rededication of the temple and its altar for eight days, and it was decreed that a similar festival be held each year, beginning on the twenty-fifth of Kislev (see 1 Macc 4:36–59). The festival remains to this day as one of the most important of Jewish feasts, not least aided by the fact that it can be held in the homes of the people. The festival was and is characterized by the use of lights (possibly due to an earlier celebration of the winter solstice). Josephus called it "the Festival of Lights," "because such a freedom shone upon us." A lampstand with eight lights was used, one candle being lighted on the first day of the festival, then another each succeeding day, until all eight were alight. Rejoicing was the keynote of the festival.

An account of Jesus in the temple at the Dedication Festival is given in John 10:22–39. It is stated that it was "winter," hence Jesus walked in Solomon's Porch, doubtless because it gave shelter from the biting wind. But it is likely that the reflection on the frosty temperature related rather to the frozen spirits of the Jewish leaders (cf. John 13:30). A great deliverance from an Antichrist was being celebrated, but a greater and more terrible power now tyrannized over the Jews, and there was no sign of salvation.

But there stood Jesus, the alleged performer of miracles, regarded by many as the Messiah, yet he didn't keep the Law! What was one to make of him? Some of the leaders therefore surrounded him and asked how long he intended to provoke them, and that he should tell them whether or not he was the Messiah. Jesus actually had never publicly claimed to be the Messiah, but much of his teaching implied it. Hence he replied to them, "I told you, and you do not believe." Nevertheless, after further conversation he stated something beyond anything they had expected: "I and the Father are one" (v 30).

It is important to observe that in the context this saying relates to the unity of the Father and the Son in the work that they do. None can snatch the sheep of Jesus out of his hand, for the Father gave them to him, and none can snatch them out of the Father's hand! Jesus and the Father are one in their work of salvation. The language nevertheless points to a unity of being, as is made plain in verse 38: The Father is in the Son and the Son in the Father.

In fury the Jews alleged that Jesus had blasphemed. He responded by citing a Scripture that sounds strange to us, but which was of deepest interest to the Jews, and which they debated at length. Psalm 82:6 reads in full:

> I said, "You are gods;
> you are all the sons of the Most High."
> But you will die like mere men;
> you will fall like every other ruler.

It is evident from John 10:36 that Jesus presupposed, if not actually cited, both clauses of the psalm. "You are gods," . . . "you are all the sons of the Most High." Jews understood well that the term "god" can be applied to others than God himself. They discussed who is meant here—Israel's judges (as representatives of the supreme Judge), or angelic beings, or the people of God.

Most rabbis concluded that it was the last, more specifically Israel gathered at Sinai to receive the Law as the covenant people of God. That is evidently assumed here; Jesus says, "the Scripture called them 'gods' to whom the word of God came" . . . (v 35). It is harmonious with the Old Testament teaching that Israel is God's (adopted) Son, as in Exod 4:22, 23: "Israel is my firstborn son, . . . Let my son go, so he may worship me." The logic of Jesus' reply to his opponents is: "If the Scripture addresses God's people as 'gods' and 'sons of God,' how can you charge the representative Son of God with blasphemy when using this language of himself?"

In fact, Jesus went further than this: he spoke of himself not simply as Messiah-Son of God but specifically as "the one whom the Father consecrated and sent into the world." In the festival that celebrated the deliverance of Israel from a destroyer of true religion and the consecration of the temple for true worship, Jesus affirmed that God had consecrated him as the Redeemer, whose deliverance issues in the kingdom of God and with it the worship of God under the new covenant. The fundamental thought is the same as that made known by Jesus at the Passover, when he spoke of himself as the new temple of God for all mankind through his death and resurrection (2:19-21). Here it gains color through its context: Jesus is the fulfillment of the Festival of the Dedication!

Our review of Jesus and the Jewish festivals shows how closely bound Jesus was to the revelation of God in the Old Testament and to the faith and worship of his people expressed in their festivals. The festivals were vivid reminders to the Jews of the experiences of God in their nation's history and of the promises of God to bring that history to a glorious destiny in the kingdom of God. As they remembered they included themselves in those experiences and those promises. In Jesus both the history and the promises came to fulfillment as he revealed in his words and deeds the kingdom of God that brings salvation—to Jews and to all nations. This teaching will have been of utmost importance to the earliest readers of the Gospels, who were in close touch with Jews who had not embraced the good news. We who belong to other times and races may also gain a securer grasp of the gospel of the kingdom as we contemplate the revelation of Jesus in the festivals of his people.

5   JESUS AND HIS OWN: THE UPPER ROOM DISCOURSES

The discourses of Jesus to his disciples, recorded in chapters 13–17, are a distinctive feature of our Gospel. Mark describes what Jesus said on that occasion in nine verses; John takes five chapters to do it—seventeen times as long! But there is a difference of method involved here. Mark tells of Jesus instructing the disciples on various occasions earlier in the ministry (see, e.g., Mark 4:10–20; 7:17–23, and especially chapter 13), but John reports none of this. He evidently reserved all the instruction of Jesus to the Twelve for the Last Supper, when Jesus will have sought to prepare his men for what lay ahead of them in the light of his death. This mode of compiling discourses of Jesus, by bringing related teaching together, was followed by all the evangelists, and it is particularly plain in Matthew's Gospel (compare, for example, Matthew 13 with Mark 4, and Matthew 24, 25 with Mark 13).

It looks as though John originally drew up chapters 13 and 14 of his Gospel as a complete discourse, since 14:31 brings it to a close. If that be so, chapters 15 and 16 were formed from the reservoir of our Lord's teaching that was available to him. It is also likely that the five passages on the Holy Spirit had earlier been brought together to tell what Jesus said about the Holy Spirit, and the evangelist set them in the discourses at appropriate points. It is a very plausible suggestion that everything that is contained in John's account of the Last Supper had been remembered and repeated many times in celebrations of the Lord's Supper, and so the whole story was eventually written up by the evangelist.

People have often expressed their surprise that no report of the words of Jesus concerning the bread and wine is given in these chapters. The explanation is probably that John was aware that all Christians knew them well, and so there was no need to repeat them; he chose to provide in these discourses an exposition of the meaning of those words of Jesus that were repeated in Christian services every Sunday.

We shall divide the discourses as follows:

The washing of the disciples' feet by Jesus and prophecy of his betrayal	13:1-30
The departure and the return of Jesus	13:31-14:31
Jesus, the True Vine	15:1-17
The opposition of the world to the church	15:18-16:4a
The ministry of the Spirit and the joy of the disciples	16:4b-33
The prayer of consecration	17:1-26

The footwashing and prophecy of betrayal

The introductory paragraph in verses 1-4 contains an extraordinary contrast between the exalted dignity of Jesus and the depths of humility to which he stooped. He had come from God and was going to God, and the Father had given him "all things," i.e., complete authority; but he stripped his clothes and put on a towel to do a slave's job! Therein was seen his love "to the limit" (v 1, rather than "love to the end").

The task of washing anybody's feet was seen by the Jews as peculiarly demeaning; it was one of the few things which the Law stated a Jewish slave should not be asked to do—it should be left to a Gentile slave. Jesus and his disciple group had been invited to use the Upper Room for this occasion. It would have been carpeted, and custom demanded that they wash their dusty feet before they occupied the room. But there was no Gentile slave, and none of the disciples were prepared to do such a thing, and so they did nothing about it. Jesus therefore took the opportunity of teaching the disciples a lesson in humility: What they were not prepared to do for one another he, their "Lord and Master," did (v 14).

It is clear, however, that there are profounder dimensions to this narrative than what lies on the surface. Peter, protesting at Jesus washing his feet, is told first that only later will he be able to understand what Jesus is doing and, secondly, that if Jesus does not wash his feet he will have no part in him.

Something extraordinarily important is entailed in this action of Jesus. The clue to its meaning is given in verse 10: "He who has bathed does not need to wash . . . but is clean all over." That is the statement in the earliest manuscripts of the Gospel of John; later manuscripts have the addition after "wash"—"except the feet." This is quite certainly due to a scribe, who thought that the washing of the feet by Jesus assumes an earlier bath. It then came to be commonly believed that the earlier bath was baptism, and the washing of the feet represented the Lord's Supper! In reality Jesus was telling Peter that what he was now doing had the meaning of a *complete* cleansing that is gained by a bath. His washing of the feet of the disciples, accordingly, is a sign of the greater cleansing that Jesus is about to achieve by his sacrificial self-giving. So he is able to say later (v 10), "you are clean," i.e., through the Word he had spoken and the action that points to the death he is about to die. That entails a deeper understanding of the example of humility that Jesus gave; it was not simply his stripping off his robe and stooping to wash disciples' feet, but his stripping off his glory with the Father and stooping to the humiliation and pain of the cross; this is, indeed, "love to the limit," and such he would have his disciples show to all.

After the footwashing, Jesus "became agitated in spirit" (v 21), clearly due to what he was about to make known to the group. "One of you will betray me." The news shocked them. Now occurs the first mention of "the disciple whom Jesus loved."

The identity of the betrayer was revealed to this disciple by Jesus handing to Judas a piece of bread dipped into the central dish on the table (cf. v 18). The action is to be interpreted as a sign of favor. Jesus offered Judas a sign of friendship, and then commanded him to do at once what he intended to do. That compelled Judas to make up his mind whether to turn from his evil plan or to reject the offer of Jesus and carry it out. Never has anyone been so completely put on the spot as Judas in that moment. He chose to open his heart to the devil and shut out the Christ of God. And so he went out. The evangelist added "and it was night," although the paschal moon shone almost as brightly as the day. The night was in the heart of Judas. It always is when his kind of bargain is made.

The departure and return of Jesus

The departure of Judas leads to an exultant cry from Jesus, in striking contrast to the anguish mentioned in verse 21. The saying reminds us of 12:23: The departure of Judas and the arrival of the Greeks to see Jesus alike signified that the beginning of the end had arrived. The "glorification" of Jesus clearly has in view his death, but 12:31, 32 indicate that it embraces his exaltation to heaven also. The crucifixion-resurrection of Jesus is an indissoluble event. God is glorified in both aspects of it, and he glorifies the Son in that he made the Son's sacrifice effective for all and raised him to be Redeemer-Lord.

It is in this context that the "new command" to love as Christ loved us is set. Note, it is a command, not a suggestion. As God laid on Israel the Law as their part of the covenant that they should be the people of God, so the Son of God, when initiating the new covenant, laid on his people one supreme command. The addition, "as I have loved you," is beyond our ability; it can be demanded only because the new covenant is characterized by grace and the gift of the Holy Spirit. The church thus becomes the People of the New Life, and its hallmark is love in the Jesus manner. As Christians fulfill their calling they show what a community of love is like, and they learn to extend that love to the world outside its borders.

Chapter 14 is occupied with the discourse of Jesus on his departure and return. The disciples at the end of chapter 13 are in a state of shock: One of them is to betray Jesus, Peter is going to deny Jesus, and Jesus is going away from them. What sort of awful crisis lies ahead of them? To that situation Jesus addresses the beautiful words of 14:1,

Do not let your hearts continually be in turmoil;
keep on believing in God, and keep on believing in me.

Yet rarely did Jesus ask so difficult a thing. They were shortly to see him arrested, ridiculed, and condemned, learn of his being flogged by Pilate's soldiers, and finally see him from a distance nailed to a cross. How should they believe in him through all that? They didn't. Only in the light of Easter were they to grasp that God's will was never more truly done than in those very events, and that in them was faith's supreme ground and inspiration.

Jesus and His Own: The Upper Room Discourses

The imagery of the departure and return of Jesus (in verses 2 and 3) is literally "homey" (the British expression is "homely"!). It makes no reference to the terrible circumstances of his "going away," i.e., through crucifixion, and none to the splendor and glory of his "coming back." It states in simplest terms that the death of Jesus is for the purpose of his securing a place in the Father's house for his followers, and that he will welcome them into it on his return.

In view of references to the "coming" of Jesus later in this discourse some scholars question whether verse 3 really has in view the coming of Christ for the victory of his kingdom, or whether it refers to his coming in some other way, perhaps through the coming of the Spirit at Pentecost, or possibly in death. To me these suggestions are very doubtful.

In verse 18, "I shall not leave you orphans, I shall come back to you," the context indicates that the reference is to Jesus coming back in the Easter resurrection. That is seen in verse 19, "After a little while the world will see me no longer, but you will see me; because I live you too will live." The thought is expounded at length in 16:16-24, which plainly has in mind the resurrection of Jesus.

In verse 23, however, a quite different thought is in view. Jesus says, "If anyone loves me he will keep my word, and my Father will love him, and we shall come to him, and we shall make our dwelling with him." That picks up the saying in verse 2, "in my Father's house there are many dwellings." Jesus goes away so that there may be a place for us in that "home," but he declares that in this time the Father and the Son will "come" to those who love him and they will make their home with them. The promise is a kind of anticipation of the coming of the Lord and the welcoming to the Father's home. The meaning of all this is perfectly clear. The Lord who departs from this earthly scene through death comes and reveals himself as the conqueror of death at Easter. He comes to every one who believes in him, so that the believer may know something of heaven on earth in this life; and he shall complete the joy of fellowship with the Father and the Spirit when he comes to bring his people home. Marvelous promises! And we know something of their fulfillment even now.

Verses 25–31 form an epilogue to the first discourse. They hark back to the beginning of chapter 14 and utter a bequest of peace. In reality that is the salvation of God. Jesus must now complete the Father's purpose, confront the devil, and win salvation for the world. Accordingly he tells his disciples, "Get up, and let us go from this place"—that is, to meet the foe. The battle must now be joined!

Jesus, the True Vine

The figure of the vine (or sometimes vineyard) is frequent in the Old Testament for Israel. It is remarkable, however, that whenever Israel is so described, the vine or vineyard is under the judgment of God for failing to produce fruit, or for producing only bad fruit (see especially Isa 5, but also Jer 2:21; Ezek 15:1–8; Ps 80:8–18). In contrast to this, Jesus is the *True* Vine; he fulfills God's purpose, not only in himself, but in those who are united with him in faith. Observe that in this figure Jesus is not said to be the trunk and believers the branches; he is the tree in which the branches live and are therefore productive. The figure is closely similar to that of Christ as the body, in whom the believers are limbs (so 1 Cor 12:12: "as the body is one . . . so it is with Christ," RSV).

In the allegory it is urged that the branches must "remain" in the vine (v 4). The reality speaks of a continuance in union with Jesus. Its meaning is spelled out in verses 7–10. It is to let his *words* remain in us—to heed them and live by them (v 7). It is to live in the *love* of Jesus (v 9), i.e., in the consciousness of his love for us, to rejoice in it and to depend upon it. It is to live in *obedience* to the Lover (v 10), since that shows the genuineness of our responsive love.

The result of such "remaining" in Jesus is fruit bearing. And "fruit" would appear to mean all the manifestations of genuine faith. Verse 16 further indicates that it includes also winning converts to Christ as the fruit of his suffering for them (". . . that you should go forth and yield fruit"). But the ultimate product of fruit bearing is love (v 17). That is the fruit that most delights the Lord.

The opposition of the world to the church

In the opening paragraph of this section causes of the world's opposition to the followers of Jesus are described: the world's hatred of Jesus is directed to those who follow him (v 18); and the disciples of Jesus, like their Lord, are not "of this world," i.e., they belong to a different world (v 19, cf. 3:31; 8:23; 18:36, 37). The world may be counted on to make a similar response to them as it did to Jesus, i.e., rejection—and yet also, in measure, acceptance (v 20).

There follows a grim warning of an increase of opposition to the disciples (16:1–4). This will lead to their exclusion from the synagogues, and even attempts to have them put to death. The first clause of verse 2 reminds us of the last beatitude of Jesus in Matt 5:11, 12, and especially its parallel in Luke 6:22, 23 (NIV): "Blessed are you when men hate you, when they exclude you and insult you and reject your name as evil, because of the Son of Man."

The second clause of verse 2 finds a remarkable illustration in the Talmud (*Num. Rab.* 21.19a): the slaying by Phineas of a Jew and of a Moabite woman with whom the man cohabited is interpreted, on the basis of Num 25:13, as an atoning sacrifice; the comment is added, "This alone will teach you that everyone who pours out the blood of the godless is like one who offers a sacrifice." The story of the Christian church, from the lynching of Stephen to the last attempt of a Roman emperor (Diocletian) to annihilate the church, along with the many attempts that have been made to do that same thing through the centuries to our own time, provides a continuous exposition of this passage.

The ministry of the Spirit and the joy of the disciples

The two longest statements relating to the Holy Spirit in the Upper Room discourses fall in this section. We shall take the opportunity to consider all five of them (14:15–17; 14:25, 26; 15:26, 27; 16:7–11, 12–15).

The first of these sayings refers to the Holy Spirit as "another Paraclete." That name is really the Greek word for the Spirit in these passages. It is often used in discussions about the Holy Spirit because it is difficult to find a real parallel for it in our language. Often it denotes a legal adviser in court, but it is not a legal term like advocate, barrister, or attorney; it can have a more general meaning like "helper." In 16:8–11 the legal associations are to the fore, and there the Spirit appears to perform the functions of a prosecuting barrister in court. But in 14:25 and 26 and 16:13 and 14 his task is to recall and interpret the revelation given through Jesus. The chief work of the Paraclete-Spirit is indicated in 15:26: "He will bear witness concerning me."

The Spirit is to "teach" and "remind" the disciples of all that Jesus said to them (14:26). These are complementary, almost identical tasks (note how remembering and understanding are closely linked in 2:17–22 and 12:16). The Spirit *teaches* as he *reminds*. Accordingly he brings no new revelation, but points to that which Jesus brought, and enables the disciples to understand it.

The Spirit will "bear witness" to Jesus, and so will the disciples (15:26 and 27). This affirmation would appear to mean that the Spirit will bear joint witness with the disciples as they proclaim Jesus in the gospel. The saying is closely parallel to Mark 13:9, 11, and the Q-saying in Luke 12:11, 12 and Matt 10:19, 20. It serves as a reminder of the context in which the early disciples frequently preached the gospel— on trial for preaching Christ! But it also indicates that the Holy Spirit is the power behind the apostolic witness to Christ: He makes it effective (cf. Mark 16:19, 20).

The Holy Spirit in his witness to Jesus will expose the world (16:8) and thereby reveal its wrong in relation to sin, righteousness, and judgment (16:9-11; for a striking example cf. Acts 24:24, 25). The emphasis on unbelief as the major sin runs through John's Gospel (cf. 1:11; 3:19; 15:22). The "world" saw in the death of Jesus proof of his *wrong*, but the Spirit is to bring home to people the fact that he was *right* (and righteous!), since his "lifting up" on the cross was one with his exaltation to the throne of God. That act, moreover, entailed the dethronement of the devil, who led the world to oppose him and put him to death. The world accordingly shared in that judgment, and its continuation in rejecting Jesus as Lord continues to implicate it in that judgment. To reveal the truth of these realities is the task of the Paraclete-Spirit.

The last Paraclete saying (16:12-15) expands what is stated in the second (14:26). The Paraclete is to guide the disciples in all the truth revealed in Jesus, a necessary process because the disciples so little grasped its depths and heights; and the church needs that ministry ever after. The Spirit teaches what he hears, just as Jesus taught what he heard from the Father; it is one revelation of God in Christ that is communicated.

A final word on the Spirit's ministry is apparently contained in 16:25. It may especially relate to verses 16-24, but it extends also to the last discourses in their entirety, and perhaps is intended to apply to the teaching of Jesus throughout his ministry. To this point Jesus has spoken

"in figures" (RSV, or "figuratively," NIV). In the language of
Jesus the word actually means "proverbs," "parables," and
"riddles"—all three; so we may understand Jesus as saying,
"I have said these things to you *in the obscure speech of
metaphor.*" But in the coming "hour," i.e., after the death
and resurrection of Jesus, he will speak *plainly* of the Father.
This must refer to his instruction of the disciples and the
church through the Holy Spirit. It is a striking promise;
along with the rest of the Paraclete sayings it found fulfillment in the Gospel in which it is set, as also in the ministry
of the Spirit as God's people have sought to understand his
Word.

The prayer of consecration

This matchless prayer is often called "the High Priestly
Prayer of Jesus." Westcott, seeing the focal point of the prayer
to be in verses 17-19, aptly named it "the Prayer of Consecration,"[1] and that title we prefer. Commonly the prayer is divided into three sections: Jesus prays for himself (vv 1-5), for
his disciples (vv 6-19), and for his church (vv 20-26). We
suggest subdividing the latter two sections, and will follow
that pattern in our exposition.

1. *Prayer for the glory of the Son, vv 1-5.* In light of 12:23,
27, 31, 32 the prayer that the Father may glorify the Son will
have in mind two things: that the death of the Son may be
an acceptable sacrifice, and that he be raised from death to
the Father's presence. With that prayer answered the kingdom of God will be opened for all believers. Such a coming
of the kingdom will issue both in the greater glory of God
and in entrance into it by the Lord's people (vv 2, 3); for
eternal life is the life of the kingdom of God in his presence
and under his gracious care.

2. *Prayer for the disciples of Jesus, vv 6-19.* (*a*) Jesus prays
for the disciples and "not for the world" (v 9). This exclusion

Jesus and His Own: The Upper Room Discourses

of the world from the prayer of Jesus must be understood in its context. The disciples have been called to continue the mission of the Lord to the world (v 18). Self-evidently this task includes mobilizing the church to engage in that mission also. It is as the church fulfills its calling that the world will recognize that Jesus has been sent to them by God (vv 21, 23). To this extent the prayer of Jesus for the disciples is indirectly prayer for the world also.

The key petition for the disciples is in verse 11: "Keep them in your name . . . that you have given me," i.e., through adherence to what Jesus has revealed to the disciples of the "name" or the character of God. It is as they are kept in adherence to that revelation that the further prayer can be answered, "that they may be one, just as we are one."

(b) A profound extension of the prayer that the disciples be "kept in your name" is made in verses 17–19: "Consecrate them in the truth. . . . For their sakes I consecrate myself, that they also may become consecrated in (the) truth." In light of the utterances of Jesus during the Supper—"this is my body . . . this is my blood . . ." (Mark 14:22, 24)—"I consecrate myself" must mean consecrate to death for the sake of humankind. The continuance of the prayer, however, "that *they* may be consecrated . . ." indicates an overlap in the meaning of the consecration of Jesus and that of his disciples.

His dedication to death is made in order that they too may be dedicated to the task of bringing the saving sovereignty to the world, and that in a like spirit as he brought it. He alone through his redemptive work can introduce God's kingdom of salvation into the world and open its gates for all; but his disciples can, and should, serve as its instruments as they proclaim the good news to the world. This they will best do as they exemplify in their own lives the suffering love of the Redeemer.

3. Prayer that all believers may be one, vv. 20–23. Here the petition of verse 11b is expanded. It is to be observed that the single prayer for the church in the world is "that they may be one." The nature of this unity is strikingly defined: "as you, Father, are in me and I am in you." It is a unity grounded in the being of God and in the redemptive action of God in Christ.

Its goal is equally profound: "that they also may be in us" (v 21); "I in them and you in me" (v 23). In the former petition the redeemed become one by participating in the fellowship of the Father and the Son; in the latter, that participation is through their union with the Son, for the Son of God is the one Mediator between God and man. Clearly, this is a unity that cannot possibly be achieved by the efforts that people—even Christian people—can make. It is the fruit of God's redemptive work in Christ. And the prayer has been answered, so surely as God answered the prayer of Jesus to glorify the Son that the Son may glorify him!

Nevertheless, it is abundantly plain that the church is called to *give expression* to this unity created by God. The unity has to become visible before the world. Accordingly Jesus prays, "that the world may believe . . . that the world may know." The church is to be the embodiment of its gospel, that the world may not only hear the good news but see its power in bringing about a community of Life and Love such as the world needs.

4. Prayer that believers may be perfected in the glory of the Son, vv 24–26. The prayer that the Lord's people may be with him and behold his glory (v 24) is without indication of time, apart from the fact that it follows his "glorification." Since, however, the prayer has the church in view, and Jesus goes to prepare a place for his own and is to return to welcome them to the Father's house (14:2, 3), it is likely that the glory of his coming and the consummation of the kingdom of God are primarily in mind.

The petition of verse 24 is grounded in verses 25 and 26. The goal of Christ's revelation of the Father's name is stated in verse 26: "that the love with which you have loved me may be in them. . . ." It has a variety of implications: an ever-increasing understanding of the love of the Father for the Son, an ever fuller grasp of the wonder that that love is extended to believers, an ever-growing love on their part to the Father, and an ever deeper fellowship with him as they abide in the Son and he in them. In this way the command to love in 13:34 attains its ultimate fulfillment, and the prayer of verse 24 its final exposition. The glory of Christ is the glory of God's love. Seen by his people, it transforms them into bearers of Christly love.

Such is the goal of history in the new creation brought about by the Son of God—Revealer and Redeemer in the past, the present, and the future.

6 THE GLORIFICATION OF JESUS

All four Gospels in the New Testament conclude with an account of the circumstances that led to the death of Jesus —his arrest and trial, his crucifixion, burial, and resurrection. And each one emphasizes certain features in the happenings of the last week of the life of Jesus. In this the fourth evangelist is no exception. He selects elements in the familiar story that serve as pointers to the meaning of the event that was to change history and determine the destiny of humankind for all time.

A primary emphasis of the evangelist in his description of the suffering of Jesus is that he who is here tried, humiliated, rejected, and crucified, is none other than God's *King*—the Lord of Israel and of the nations. No account is given of the trial of Jesus before the supreme court of the Jews, the Sanhedrin (contrast Mark 14:53–64 and parallels). That Jesus was brought for trial before the Sanhedrin under the leadership of Caiaphas is presumed to be known. John's concern is limited to the trial of Jesus by Pilate, and the governor's dealings with Jesus and with the Jewish leaders, for in these the primary issues of the life and death of Jesus are most clearly seen.

The Glorification of Jesus

The first utterance of Pilate to Jesus is a question, "Are you the king of the Jews?" (John 18:33). The question itself assumes what had taken place in the Jewish trial, notably the high priest's question ("Are you the Messiah?") and Jesus' answer ("I am . . . ," Mark 14:61, 62). The translation of Messiah as King of the Jews was easy enough, but it placed Jesus in a situation of *lèse majesté*, i.e., of committing high treason, for Caesar alone could be recognized as king of the Jews (see John 19:15).

The answer of Jesus was first a negative statement as to the nature of his kingdom: It is not a kingdom of this world, the kind of kingdom Pilate serves. That leads inevitably to a second question of Pilate: "So then you *are* a king?" That elicits a positive statement from Jesus: His kingdom is the kingdom of truth. He was born and came into the world to bear witness to this kingdom. For the kingdom of truth is none other than the kingdom of salvation.

The answer of Jesus led Pilate to make an abortive attempt to release Jesus, but the Jewish leaders and the crowd gathered with them called for the release of Barabbas instead. Pilate therefore handed Jesus over to the soldiers that they should flog him. Why was this done? In all likelihood, in hope of satisfying the Jews with a lesser punishment than the ultimate one of death. The flogging, however, as practiced by Romans was of appalling severity, frequently capable of killing a victim. This is to be borne in mind in the subsequent narrative; Jesus will have been in a condition of near physical collapse, and it will have been apparent to all.

Nevertheless, the soldiers were not finished with Jesus after his flogging. They wove a crown of long thorns, to imitate a crown of a divine king, and clothed him with a purple coat, then gave him the kind of salutation they accorded to the Roman emperor ("Hail, king of the Jews!" is said in imitation of the cry, "Hail, Caesar!"). John records the soldiers' cruel action, but not simply to show a sadistic act of mockery; like Caiaphas, the soldiers said better than they knew. Jesus is God's king, and warrants more truly than Caesar the homage of all humankind.

When the soldiers took Jesus back to the governor, dressed as a parody of a king, Pilate promptly led Jesus out to the crowd and cried, "Look, the Man!" It is improbable that this was done for spite. More likely it was to make Jesus appear as a pitiful figure who was plainly no danger to Romans or Jews, and so to persuade the Jewish leaders to agree to release him.

The evangelist, of course, will have had other thoughts in recording this. For him Pilate's cry was a call to look at *the Man sent from God*, whose majesty was veiled by sacrificial love and whose suffering was the means of bringing the kingdom of salvation for all people, including those thirsting for his blood and those who were shedding it.

Pilate's ploy failed. He therefore took his place on the judgment seat. Jesus will have been made to stand beside him. The crowd awaited the sentence of judgment. Instead, to their astonishment, Pilate called out to them, "Look, your king!" He made the moment of Jesus' condemnation the occasion for declaring his kingship. In so doing he confronted the Jews with a momentous decision: were they willing to send their king to death, or did they wish to relent? This latter course they were unwilling to take. On the contrary, they committed the greatest act of apostasy in Jewish history: they declared, "We have no king except Caesar." In light of Jesus' proclamation of the kingdom of God, that was tantamount to a rejection of the reason for Israel's existence. After that there was no more to be said. The King of the Jews was sent to the gallows.

The last word, however, was not with the Jewish leaders but with Pilate. It was customary for a condemned criminal to have a card round his neck, stating the crime for which he was to die. Jesus was made to wear just such a placard. The wording was, "Jesus the Nazarene, the King of the Jews," and it was written in multiple languages so that all who saw could understand. It was Pilate's act of revenge on the Jewish leaders. They controlled their fury and asked that he add a single word to the card, namely, "I am" (that is one word in the languages used). The addition would have meant that Jesus claimed to be king, but that he was a liar. Pilate refused to change the inscription, and in so doing refused to change the truth into a lie. Jesus died as King of the Jews—rejected by those who should have owned him, but appointed by God as the King who saves alike Jews and people of every nation under heaven.

Of the rest of the story of the last hours of Jesus on the cross there is one happening to which the evangelist attached greatest importance. Joseph of Arimathea, a member of the Jewish Sanhedrin, requested of Pilate that he might give Jesus a proper burial (i.e., not one in a common grave, as the Jewish leaders had in view, 19:31). This he was permitted to do.

He and Nicodemus accordingly prepared the body of Jesus for burial. Joseph supplied the grave clothes, Nicodemus the spices, but the evangelist notes that Nicodemus supplied a prodigious quantity—one hundred liters of spices. In today's measures that represents sixty-five and a half pounds, an enormous amount to use on one individual. The only people recorded as receiving such a burial were kings. One may compare what happened at the burial of King Asa, recorded in 2 Chr 16:14. At the funeral of Herod the Great spices were carried by hundreds of slaves. More to the point, it is stated that Onkelos, a contemporary of our evangelist, at the death of Gamaliel the Elder burned eighty liters of spices. When asked why he had done so he cited the words of Jeremiah (34:4–5) to king Zedekiah: "You shall die in peace, and with the burnings in honor of your fathers (i.e., earlier kings) who were before you," and he added, "Is not Rabbi Gamaliel far better than a hundred kings?"[1] Doubtless Nicodemus, if he had been similarly questioned, would have answered in a like spirit, "Is not Jesus far greater than all kings?"

The death of Jesus as the king who brings the kingdom of salvation to the world has various important aspects to which John draws attention. The last word of Jesus on the cross of which he knows is his cry, "It is accomplished!" (19:30). The utterance indicates not alone that the earthly work of Jesus has now come to an end, but that the task assigned him has been accomplished. If we ask what it is that has been accomplished, and allow Jesus to answer for himself, we must say, "Nothing less than the judgment of the world!" So Jesus declared in anticipation of his hour (12:31). In the murder of the Son of God sin has been revealed as a God-opposing force that is God-destructive in its intent. But the unique and astonishing feature of the death of Jesus is that in the event wherein the world sought to destroy him, God gave his Son that the world might not perish! The Son of God endured the judgment of God that should have fallen on the would-be destroyers of God!

In virtue of Jesus, the Son of God, bearing the judgment of God upon the world two immense consequences follow. First, Satan has no ground of accusing humanity represented by the Mediator; he has been "thrown out" of heaven and so has no access before God in heaven (John 12:31; the imagery is comparable to that in Job chs 1, 2). This is a vivid way of saying that sinful man is justified in Christ, and the decision cannot be reversed by any accuser (cf. Rom 8:33, 34).

Secondly, the Mediator is exalted from his cross to the right hand of God. The vaunted "prince of this world" has been dethroned and the Christ of God enthroned. In the dying and rising of the King of Israel the kingdom of God has come in fullness of blessing to humankind, he is revealed as Lord and Savior of the nations, and the doors of the kingdom have been opened for all who own him as Redeemer.

This fundamental understanding of the saving work of

Jesus is represented by the evangelist through a symbol that appears throughout his Gospel, namely, that of a second Exodus that brings freedom, not for one nation but for all nations. John, and John alone, records a request of the Jewish leaders that the men who had been crucified on that day should not be left to hang on the crosses, eventually to be devoured by vultures, but rather that they be killed and buried speedily, so that the land should not be defiled by the corpses during the Passover (John 19:31). This request was granted. Soldiers were sent to hasten the death of the crucified men.

As we have noted, the soldiers did this to the two men beside Jesus, and were about to do the same to him when they saw that he was dead already. There was no need therefore to smash the legs of Jesus, but one soldier thrust his spear into his side, presumably to make sure that he was truly dead.

This happening was observed by an eyewitness and through him was made known to the evangelist, who saw it as deeply significant. These events happened, he affirmed, "that the Scripture might be fulfilled, 'Not a bone of his is to be broken,' and again another Scripture says, 'They will look on him whom they pierced.'" There is no doubt as to the primary reference the evangelist had in view in this passage: The Passover Festival is about to be celebrated, the Passover lambs have been slaughtered (at the time when Jesus was crucified!), and his executioners were restrained from smashing his bones. Jesus accordingly dies as the Lamb of God, fulfilling the meaning and the hope of Passover, and bringing about the "redemption" of the world, i.e., real freedom, liberation, emancipation, and an Exodus from the powers of sin and death for life in the kingdom of God under the Savior Christ.

In view of the evangelist's fundamental assumption of the unity of the death and resurrection of Jesus, it is to be expected that some light on the Lord's saving work should be shed by the resurrection narratives. In this we are not disappointed. After the preliminary accounts of the finding of the empty tomb and the appearance of the risen Lord to Mary Magdalene, the essential meaning of the resurrection of Jesus is concentrated into a single short paragraph, John 20:19–23.

The first words of the risen Lord to the disciples gathered in the Upper Room are "Peace to you!" or, in the language he had always used with his disciples, "Shalom!" Everybody knows that that term was and is the everyday greeting of Jews in Palestine. But the occasion of this use of it was far from everyday. Shalom is the most comprehensive word for salvation in the Old Testament. Primarily it denotes well-being, health, completeness, prosperity, a relation of friendship with others and so in a wider context absence of war; most of all, however, it denotes a happy relationship with God and the world which he alone can establish.

In the writings of the prophets peace is the gift of God which his people will know in the kingdom of God. The prophecy of the coming of the Messiah in Micah 5:2–5 concludes with the famous words:

> He will stand and shepherd his flock
> in the strength of the Lord,
> in the majesty of the name of the Lord his God.
> And they will live securely, for then his greatness
> will reach to the ends of the earth.
> And he will be their peace. (NIV)

When, therefore, the Lord, after his crucifixion and resurrection, uttered the greeting to his disciples, "Shalom to you," it carried a fullness of meaning such as it had never borne on the lips of any man. All the prophetic anticipations of the blessings of the kingdom of God had essentially been realized in the living, dying, and rising of Jesus. His "Shalom" of

Easter evening is the complement of "It is finished" on the cross, for the peace of reconciliation with God and man was achieved and was now imparted.

The joy of the disciples was a natural response to the sight of their beloved Lord, an overwhelming gladness to see him alive after the appalling death that he had suffered (John 20:20). Later, their joy was to be deepened as they came to realize the profound significance of the Easter events. For joy is an inseparable concomitant of the kingdom of God (as may be seen in such typical passages as Isa 25:6–9 and Rev 21:2–4). Paul reflects precisely this consciousness when he defined the kingdom of God as "righteousness, peace, and joy in the Holy Spirit" (Rom 14:17).

The accomplishment of the salvation of the kingdom of God by the crucified and risen Lord is accompanied by a commission to make the good news known. The Lord's "Shalom to you" is to be proclaimed to every creature under heaven, and that in the Jesus manner. So it is that in our Gospel the great commission runs, "As the Father has sent me, I also am sending you" (John 20:21). In these words there is a reflection of a principle of representation that was fundamental to the Jewish people: "One who is sent is as he who sends him." It finds expression in the saying of Jesus in John 13:20, "He who receives anyone I send receives me, and he who receives me receives the One who sent me" (cf. Matt 10:40 and Luke 10:16).

Just as Jesus was sent as the representative of the Father, and taught and acted with the authority of God, so the disciples are sent as the representatives of Jesus to make known the kingdom of God with the authority and power vested in him. The followers of Jesus, however, are expected to observe the way he exercised his authority. For he was sent to fulfill the vocation of the Servant of the Lord, in a spirit of humility and obedience to the Father, as set forth in the songs of the Servant in Isaiah 42–53. So also the servants of the Servant of the Lord are to go in like manner, embodying the message they proclaim in their living. The principle is set forth in words that need to be pondered by every servant of the Lord: "The Son of man also (i.e., he as well as his followers) came not to be served but to serve, and to give his life as a ransom for many" (Mark 10:45 RSV). The balance between authority and humble service is difficult to achieve, but the secret was demonstrated by the King on his way to the cross; as the ancients used to say, "He reigns from the tree."

It is important to observe that when the Son was sent forth on his mission by the Father he was conscious that he had not left the Father's presence: "He who sent me is with me," he said (John 8:29). His ministry was a partnership with the Father, aided by the Holy Spirit, the reality of which was demonstrated by the compassion and power in which he labored. So also the representatives of Jesus are sent out as partners with him in their mission. The risen Lord goes with those he sends (cf. the ending of the Great Commission in Matthew, "Look, I am with you to the end of the age!" Matt 28:20).

This authority and power of the partnership of the disciples with their Lord is expressed in a graphic manner in John's narrative. Having commissioned the disciples, the Lord said, "Receive (the) Holy Spirit" (John 20:22). The account is plainly symbolic. The unusual use of the word "he breathed in them" is reminiscent of its use in Gen 2:7, where we read, "God breathed into the nostrils of Adam the breath of life," and again in Ezek 37:9, 10 (NIV), where the prophet is bidden to call on the wind, "Breathe into these slain, that they may live." We are meant to understand by this symbolic action that the risen Lord imparted to his disciples the Holy Spirit of the new creation, which had been brought into being through his death and resurrection; thereby he enabled the service of the kingdom of God to be carried out in the power of the Holy Spirit of the kingdom. From this moment on, the partnership of the Paraclete-Spirit and the disciples begins, so fulfilling the promises of Jesus in John 14–16 concerning the sending of the Spirit.

The salvation of the kingdom of God brought into being by the crucified and risen Redeemer is no merely private enjoyment of forgiveness of sins and new life from the Lord. It is a salvation for the forgiveness and life of all humankind. With the grace of life is given the grace to communicate it. So surely as we who believe have received the former, so surely are we intended to experience the latter. When the Church engages in its mission in that faith, the reality of the partnership of the Lord of the kingdom with his subjects is seen in the transformation of men and women by the gospel of the kingdom. In that spirit, let us go to it!

NOTES

Chapter 1 Interpreting the Gospel of John

1. Reported by Eusebius, *History of the Church*, 3.31,3.

2. *Against Heresies*, 3.1,2.

3. The development of this prayer and its application to Christians have been widely discussed. For its wording and meaning see J. Jocz, *The Jewish People and Jesus Christ* (London: SPCK, 1949), 51–57. For its possible application in the fourth Gospel see *History and Theology in the Fourth Gospel*, J. L. Martyn, ed. (Nashville: Abingdon, 1979), 24–62, and especially the magisterial treatment of the subject by W. Horbury, "The Benediction of the Minim and Early Jewish-Christian Controversy," *JTS* 33 (1982): 19–61.

4. See J. Louis Martyn's treatment of this idea in *History and Theology in the Fourth Gospel*, 24–62.

5. *The Fourth Gospel* (London: Faber and Faber, 1943), 362.

6. *The Historical Jesus in the Gospel of St. John* (London: Burns and Oates, 1967), 46.

Chapter 2 The Word Made Flesh

1. *Le quatrième Evangile* (Paris: 1903), 98.

2. Hoskyns, *The Fourth Gospel*, 162.

3. *Hebrew Thought Compared with Greek* (Philadelphia: Westminster, 1960), 58–59.

4. *The Interpretation of the Fourth Gospel* (Cambridge: The University Press, 1953), 284.

5. Ibid., 285.

6. *The Gospel of John* (Oxford: Blackwell, 1971), 31.

7. *The Gospel of John*, 449.

8. *The Gospel According to John*, The Anchor Bible vol. 1 (New York: Doubleday, 1966), 535.

Chapter 3   The Signs of Jesus and their Significance

1. *The Interpretation of the Fourth Gospel*, 383–86.

2. See the Jewish Midrash, *Genesis Rabba*, 11.8c.

3. *The Gospel According to John*, vol. 2, (New York: Seabury, 1980), 335.

Chapter 4   Jesus and the Jewish Festivals

1. *The Fourth Gospel*, 281.

2. *Das Evangelium nach Johannes*, in *Erläuterungen zum Neuen Testament* (Stuttgart: Calwer Verlag, 1947), 116.

3. The Talmudic tractate *Sanhedrin*, 99a.

Chapter 5   Jesus and His Own: The Upper Room Discourses

1. *The Gospel According to St. John*, vol. 2 (London: John Murray, 1908), 238–39.

Chapter 6   The Glorification of Jesus

1. The rabbinic work *Semahoth*:8.

INDEX OF SCRIPTURES

Index of Scriptures